DIGITAL PERSONAL BRANDING

DIGITAL PERSONAL BRANDING

The Essential Guide to Online Personal Branding in the Digital Age

DARIO SIPOS

DIGITAL PERSONAL BRANDING

The Essential Guide to Online Personal Branding in the Digital Age

© 2021, Dario Sipos

The moral rights of the author have been asserted.

All rights reserved. No part of this publication may be reproduced, stored in a retrieval system, or transmitted, in any form or by any means – electronic, mechanical, photocopy, recording, scanning, or other, except for brief quotations in critical reviews or articles, without the prior written permission of the author.

Published in the European Union by DWR Ltd. (*www.dwr-eu.eu*)

ISBN 978-953-49031-3-1 (paperback)
ISBN 978-953-49031-4-8 (ebook)
ISBN 978-953-49031-5-5 (hardcover)

Table of Contents

DARIO SIPOS IS A DIGITAL marketing strategist, branding expert, keynote public speaker, business columnist and author of *Digital Retail Marketing*. He has built his unique skill set during 10+ years of experience working in every aspect of digital marketing. He has spent significant time working all over the world in the digital field, helping clients, and developing brands.

When you gain online influence, you have the ability to transform minds, behaviors, and outcomes. Dario will help you become an influential presence on the Internet, which means that people will respect your opinions, trust your judgment, and listen to your voice above all others.

Dario helps leaders influence positive outcomes in all directions, even under the most difficult and changing conditions.

To find out more about Dario and his journey, follow him at:

www.dariosipos.com

INTRODUCTION:

THE FUTURE OF HUMAN EXISTENCE – YOU ARE WHAT YOU SAY YOU ARE

Everything not saved will be lost.
                              Nintendo "Quit Screen" Message

WHEN YOU MEET A SMART, ambitious person who presents ideas well but, despite all that, does not progress in their career, most likely they do not have a well-established personal brand.

In the entire world today, there are two types of people: The ones that comprehend the benefits of personal branding and the ones that consider it mindless bragging.

Personal branding does not mean sharing your private or uninteresting and irrelevant information; instead, it means sharing accurate, credible information about how you bring value to the world. Successful branding is based on authenticity with an element of aspiration toward future success. At the same time, simplicity is the key to effective messaging.

When you are aiming for your next career goal, having the right skills and working hard count for nothing if no one can envisage you in that bigger role. The new business world does not take the time or have the patience to discover your real value; instead, you need to be intentionally delivering, building, and cultivating your personal brand.

Personal branding is not a new thing, yet until recently it was only used by the few who were ready to tread that path before the rest of the world.

As you are bombarded every day with endless ads, emails, and social media messaging, you might get the impression that you cannot possibly create your personal brand in that vast crowd. Actually, that conclusion is entirely wrong, and it would be an incorrect assumption just to stay completely quiet. When you use them correctly, digital marketing tools will lift you above the crowd and get you noticed.

Most people connect personal branding with bragging; actually, your personal branding is simply telling the world how you deliver value to it.

In a range of professions, and especially for those who work remotely, digital personal branding is crucial to demonstrate your value and remain in line for new projects, promotions, responsibilities.

Personal branding is for everyone, not just famous, well-connected individuals. Personal branding is not complex, yet it requires effort. Fifty percent of personal branding success is born out of consistency and maximizing the opportunities that materialize in front of you. The famous business consultant Brian Tracy formulates the secret to success: "Fifty percent of success is getting in the line of success, another fifty percent is remaining in the line of success".

If you do not build and improve your own brand, then the people around you do it for you, which means your complete future is in other people's hands. To succeed in your career, you shouldn't let others build your personal brand. To keep our reputation in order, we must manage our personal brands.

There isn't a more public expression of our personal brand than a digital online presence. Inevitably our digital presence is going to be used as part of the equation to establish our eligibility to be accepted to jobs, universities, and various networking opportunities.

Occasionally googling yourself to see how you show up online becomes necessary because Google results are your first impression for your job interviews and meetings. People will research you online whenever they want to learn about you. The Internet is the first place where we go when we want to learn more about anything or anyone.

If the search engine doesn't find you, there is a void that is almost like you do not exist. Without anything to confirm your credibility, your reputation suffers. Anonymity and mistaken identity are real threats to your reputation, while sharing factual information about your personal brand is not a risk at all. It's your opportunity to share information about yourself that you want, instead of relying on search engines to connect the dots, which can mean you don't appear at all or someone mistaken as you appears instead.

The benefit of digital personal branding is that all published information remains online, usually, for a very long time, which is essential in the world of information overload where everything not saved gets lost.

The perception of your digital personal brand is your reality. What people perceive about you when you post and interact online becomes your reality. If people perceive you as good in your field of work, they will be more likely to hire you. By changing an audience's perception, you can create a new reality for yourself.

Personal branding online is not about pretending to be a perfect person. It is about being authentic in the world with all your strengths – and flaws.

The reputation of a person is other people's subjective perception of their attributes. Reputation evolves over time, but it can be engineered. On the Internet, which is an extensive network, it's easier to change reputation than it is in a small group circle because people depend on search engines, like Google, to make decisions for them – including about other people's reputations.

To develop and grow your brand, you need to create a strategy with a serious approach because there is no other brand that you will work on more important than your own brand.

The goal of your digital personal branding is to show your identity, represent your current achievements, and present yourself as the person that you want to become. In the online world, the rule is that you are what you say you are.

Personal brands are best tested when you leave the room. What do people say when you are not there?

When you have an effective personal brand, people will recognize you as a "specialist" in your field. When you have a digital personal brand then you have online influence, which means you have the ability to transform minds, behaviors, and outcomes.

Having a digital personal brand enables you to craft an online persona that reflects your personal values and professional skills. Even with occasional moderate use, the content you create, share, or engage with will build your personal brand's public narrative. How you behave online is now as important as your offline behavior.

By reading this book, you will learn how to build your own brand using new rules and tools so you can achieve your goals in life and your career. You will fully understand what it means to build a digital personal brand, realizing that it was much easier than you ever expected.

You already have a personal brand, so you do not need to create it; all you need to do is make it stronger and make it digital. The best time to develop your personal digital brand is today.

CHAPTER 1

PERSONAL BRAND IN A DIGITAL AGE

Personal Branding is the art of becoming knowable, likable, and trustable.

John Jantsch

DEFINITION OF DIGITAL PERSONAL BRANDING

Personal branding is the process of communicating your value to the community, while digital personal branding simply uses online tools to do it more effectively.

Whether you like it or not, you already have a personal brand because people categorize you based on their perceptions. The question is if you are branded as the person that brings value or if you rely on people to brand you as they wish.

The majority of people think that personal branding is self-bragging and is, therefore, selfish and not a polite thing to do.

The point of personal branding is to make your life better. When other people make crucial decisions about you and your life (for example, a new job or promotion), they are considering your personal brand and it's a major deciding factor. You should have your personal brand ready for inspection at any moment because it is checked daily by your colleagues, bosses, and business partners.

At all times, you need to make sure that your personal brand has entirely accurate information and fix any gap; for example, fix a lack of experience in any relevant area simply by educating yourself more.

What is your personal brand?

1. **Personal brand is how others view you**
   The vast majority of people, especially at work, already have a very defined view of you. You create that view in the form of your values, character, how you work, what you focus on, and what you are good at. All that is an accumulation of your interaction with your environment.

2. **Personal brand is your reputation**
   The reputation of a personal brand is a generalization of how your audience views you. It is how your audience understands and brings together your traits and character.

3. **Personal brand is your uniqueness**
   Most people don't feel their work is unique because many others do the same or similar work. A combination of elements creates uniqueness while it doesn't mean "one of a kind". It instead means those things that are unique to you because of your experiences, skills, education, character, or values.

4. **Personal brand is how your audience values you**
   Suppose your audience at work always asks for your help with a particular issue or query. In this case, they consider your expertise valuable on a specific topic. This happens because you created that perception by talking, achieving, and demonstrating your ability to help at a particular thing. Managers tend to promote individuals who provide the greatest value to them.

5. **Personal brand is what people expect from you**
   Your reputation creates expectations within your audience. When you have a personal brand, it summarizes – in effect – what your contribution will be to your audience, so you do not need to explain it. Your reputation precedes you.

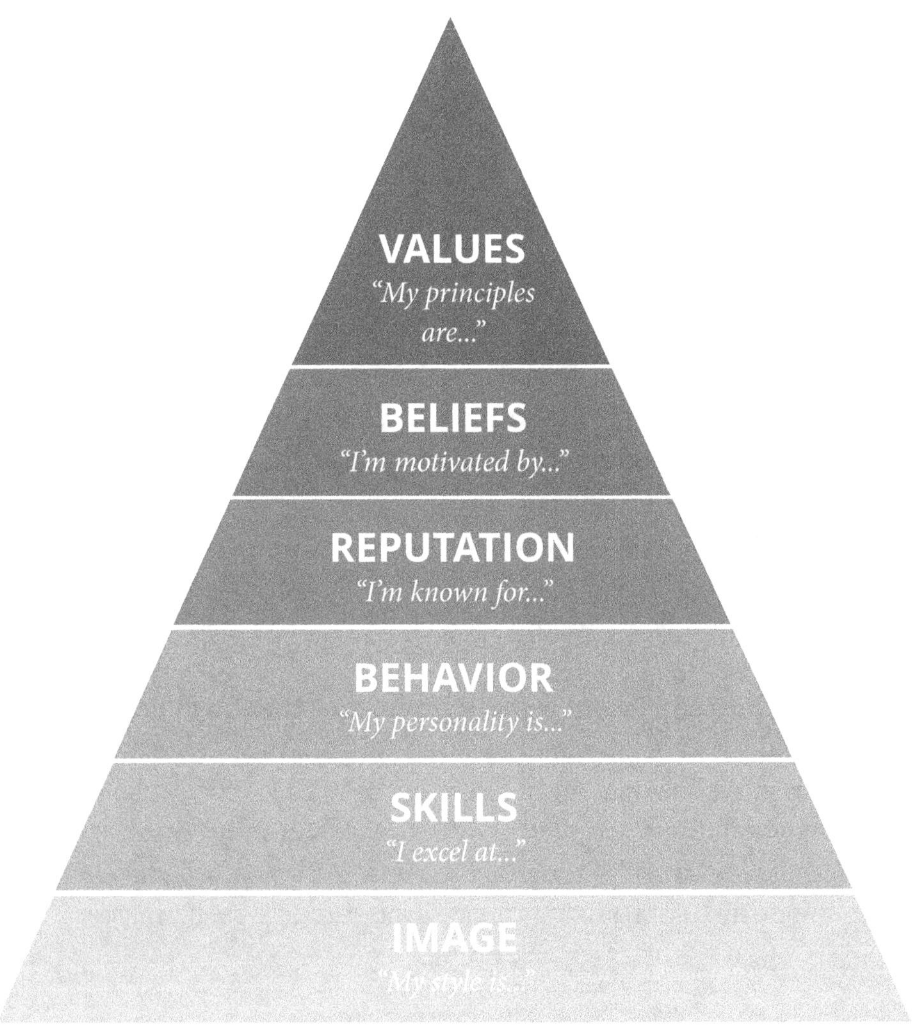

Figure 1. Personal Brand Pyramid

MYTHS OF PERSONAL BRANDING

The most common misconception is that doing great work will result in an excellent personal reputation. The world has no way of knowing about your great work unless you inform them about it. Another common misconception is thinking that company management will notify the world of your outstanding value contribution. The biggest misconception is that personal branding is self-promotion, often in the form of mindless bragging. When done correctly, personal branding is educating the target audience on the value that you bring to the world.

The number one obstacle in personal branding is the fear of doing it, based on lack of knowledge and how to do personal branding properly.

Personal branding is not about being famous. It is about being known in specific fields by the value you bring. It means being known in a particular community so you can reach your goals.

Most people have adverse reactions to the idea that they should ever promote themselves. The negative responses arise due to the extreme examples of selfless self-promotion that we observe around us.

Here is a list of the ten most common personal branding myths:

1. **I don't have a personal brand**
   The reality is that every human already has a personal brand, merely by existing.

2. **The company brand is more important than my personal brand**
   In reality, businesses that use the founder's and employees' personal brands to their advantage attract more quality employees and customers. Business owners often make the mistake of thinking their private brand doesn't matter so much as the company brand.

3. **Personal branding is for job-seekers and salespeople**
   Even the people who do not work directly in sales are selling themselves daily as worthy colleagues or employees to companies, bosses, and colleagues. Having a personal brand developed enables us never to have to sell ourselves again.

4. **Personal branding is not for introverts**
   This would only hold true if personal branding were quantified by the number of people you interact with daily. Personal Branding is about building credibility, clarity, and consistency.

5. **Personal branding requires inventing an identity**
   Quite the opposite. Branding is based on authenticity; therefore, personal branding is about authentically communicating what your identity is.

6. **Personal branding is about bragging**
   No matter how good you are at your work, if your personal brand doesn't support that then you will not be successful. Personal branding requires a balance of adding value to the world and communicating it.

7. **Personal branding is the latest phenomenon that will pass**
   The tradition of branding has been established a long time. It is going nowhere and will become even more critical with the further development of a digitally connected world.

8. **Personal branding is a good thing while not necessary**
   In the digital world, where anyone is gaining information with a few clicks of the mouse button, neglecting digital branding will limit people's potential.

9. **Personal branding is about managing your image**
   Branding doesn't have much to do with dress sense or what car you drive. Personal branding values the person inside and what you bring to the world. Never will unfavorable business decisions be reversed just because someone at the meeting liked how you dressed or the car you arrived in.

10. **Personal branding is hard and time-consuming**
    When done correctly, personal branding is a fun activity on which you need to spend five minutes every day once your strategy and system are created. It also opens new opportunities for you, expanding the network of your contacts effortlessly.

A Brief History of Branding

Branding has a very long history, it existed in almost all the cultures around the world in some form from beginning of civilization. The oldest generic brand, in continuous use in India since ca. 1100 B.C.E to 500 B.C.E, is the herbal paste named Chyawanprash, consumed for its purported health benefit. In between the years 500–1000 C.E., the word "brand" was derived from the word "*brandr*" (originating from the ancient North Germanic Old Norse language), which means "to burn". Referring to parties and companies that were burning their brand on their products. Around the year 1500, the term "brand" is used for cattle identification. Historical evidence of old Egyptian monuments 4000 years-old show branded cattle, which establishes the concept of branding as a form of identification firmly in the ancient past.

In the year 1870, it was possible to register a trademark to prevent other businesses from using logos that were not theirs. The personal branding concept was first introduced in the year 1937 in the book *Think and Grow Rich* by Napoleon Hill. In the 1980s, branding becomes a focus point to corporations, moving corporate branding in the direction of creating culture. In the year 1982, the book *The Battle for Your Mind* by Jack Trout and Al Ries suggests "You can benefit by using positioning strategy to advance your own career. Key principle: Don't try to do everything yourself. Find a horse to ride."

The first direct use of the term "personal branding" was made by Tom Peters in his 1997 article "The Brand Called You," which presents branding in the "Age of the Individual". In the book by William Bridges, *Creating You & Co.: Learn to Think Like the CEO of Your Own Career*, it is noted that you are directing your career path.

Brands are always trying to get closer to humans and connect with them because they try to mimic human behavior of communication.

Branding used to be a tool for companies to distinguish products. Currently, brands are ways to communicate to the world who companies are and which set of values they represent.

Brands are evaluated by the worst and the best things they did for people. When you do not fit people's expectations, in most cases, it makes them upset. While in return, you gain attention based on people thinking you are unique.

The Benefits of Digital in Personal Branding

Personal branding is the process of developing a strategy and conducting a strategic action plan to develop your personal brand.

Having a strong personal brand for professionals is the way to influence and gain more opportunities. For a graduate, a personal brand is all the difference **between** getting a job or not. Entrepreneurs with a developed personal brand will bring **in** more business. They will, in that way, also encourage more quality employees to join their companies.

If your current brand is not bringing you career progress, you need to develop a better brand.

If you have a strong personal brand, which is well defined online, you can connect and communicate with the people who do not know you in person. Personal branding draws attention to what you do and what you represent so that people can find your message and communicate with you.

The difference between humans and brands is that humans are relatable. Personal branding is not about you. It is about the people you are influencing and getting your message to them. To influence the people and get your message to them, you need to use third-party authorities because people will not always listen to you immediately, but they will listen to third-party authorities (media, corporations, executives, influencers).

Personal branding will make you more humanly relatable and authentic. To succeed, you need to access the public strategically. At present times everyone has access to free digital tools useful for personal branding.

A personal brand is a hundred percent based on the opinion of others. Personal branding is for the people that desire freedom and not for the ones that want power.

When you have a strong personal brand, opportunities will arise more, such as projects, jobs, media, and speaking opportunities. The system/environment in which you live and work when you have a personal brand will automatically advocate you because it is in the system's interest. When you live your desired brand, you will feel happier in life and work.

Until the last decade, most first impressions were created in the real world at a first meeting. After that, people would research on the Internet to learn about who they have met. The situation today is quite different because the meeting is no longer where the first impression is formed. The present reality is that you need to be focused on your digital brand because that is what creates your first impression.

Before meeting you in person, people will research you online and base their impressions and decisions on what Google, LinkedIn, and other social networks display.

Suppose you do not show in the Google results. In this case, you do not exist, which creates a risk you will be misjudged or your identity mistaken.

CREATING YOUR PERSONAL BRAND

The basis of your personal brand is the person you are, the value you provide to society; therefore, your authenticity is the solid base on which you build. From authenticity, you develop your trustable identity and are easier to understand and relate to. It is from the authenticity that you connect with people on a human level.

The process of determining your authenticity is identifying your values, passions, skills, and strengths.

The general process of personal brand development can be described in the following stages:

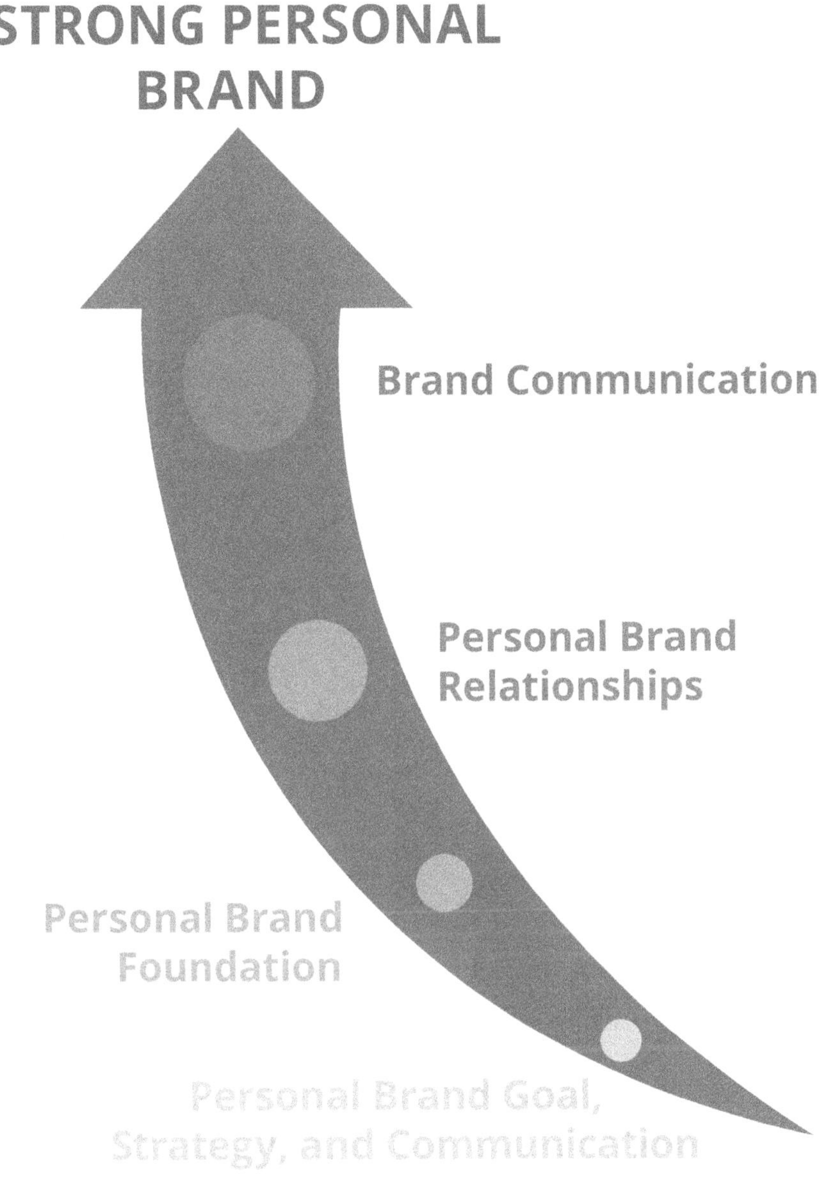

Figure 2. Elements combining strong personal brand

Personal Brand Goal, Strategy, and Communication
Knowing your current position and what you want to accomplish. Creating positioning, communication, and strategy on how to achieve goals.

Personal Brand Foundation
Deciding on which areas you need to invest in creating the foundation of your desired personal brand to deliver your value.

Personal Brand Relationships
Developing relationships with individuals that have credibility and are already influencing the opinion of others on social media.

Brand Communication
Communicating about your brand effectively and consistently. Having a solid visible brand will help you in every area of your life.

A personal brand involves continuously evolving and upgrading on your recent achievements. As the digital environment in which you build your digital personal brand evolves due to technology improvements, you need to re-evaluate in which stage you are and adjust accordingly. That practically means continuously searching for new, better ways to communicate your brand and checking if the technology invented new, more efficient channels for communication.

THE 7CS OF PERSONAL DIGITAL BRANDING

We can explain personal branding using a similar model to the seven elements of the marketing mix initially published by E. Jerome McCarthy in the 1960s because good visual representations often show themselves as the most practical way to clarify interconnected concepts.

Figure 3. The 7Cs of Personal digital branding

Character
The personal brand starts with a person behind it, an authentic character with visions, goals, talents, skills, and a voice to tell its personal or professional story. Each person in the world is the character of their own branding story.

Credibility
Over time with actions, trust is turned into credibility. The audience knows the value that your character is delivering consistently.

Channels

Channels are places where your messages reach the audience. Channels in digital personal branding are not only social media but also many other digital channels where your audience can interact with you.

Content

Content in personal branding are messages that your character is sending through digital channels to reach your target audience. It is most effective in any online channel to use rich content media, incorporating images, audio, and video.

Contacts

Contacts are the people that will like or interact with your content that you distribute to them through digital channels. It creates the network of the people that like your value and where all your future potential is evaluated.

Consistency

Consistency is the process that you need to take care of, especially when developing your personal brand—consistently reflecting your character at a determined frequency. Patience, persistence, and reliability are the key elements of creating your personal brand online.

Confirmation

It is the confirmation of others expressed by engagement with your communication and your content that serves as affirmation of your value in the community you serve. Engagement of your brand through consistent content is the confirmation you receive from your contacts that will build up your strong personal brand.

As we progress through the chapters, all the subjects involved in digital personal branding will become clearer with actionable steps you can implement in your own digital personal branding. No one can tell your story better than you can.

You will be entirely ready to start and run your digital personal branding and marketing processes continuously and consistently.

Let us dive deeper into the psychology behind personal branding.

CHAPTER 2.

PSYCHOLOGY BEHIND PERSONAL BRANDING

If you don't build a personal brand, someone else will brand you with the wrong label.

Richie Norton

PSYCHOLOGY OF INFLUENCER MARKETING

Understanding some of the psychological effects that influence social media users and all means of digital communication will help us decode most of the population's biases and preferences towards ways of communication in the real and online world.

Influencer marketing is successful because it plays directly into humans' natural desire for belonging and social conformity norms. People accept influencer marketing more than any other because it is more authentic and relatable than any other type of marketing.

People who have grown up with advertising have learned how to tune it out, which is especially the case on internet browsers where addons can turn off advertising completely. Influencer marketing can still reach those audiences by making use of the following psychological effects:

* Authority and expertise
* Halo effect
* Information over'load
* Social distance
* Social proof

INFLUENCER TRUST EXCHANGE

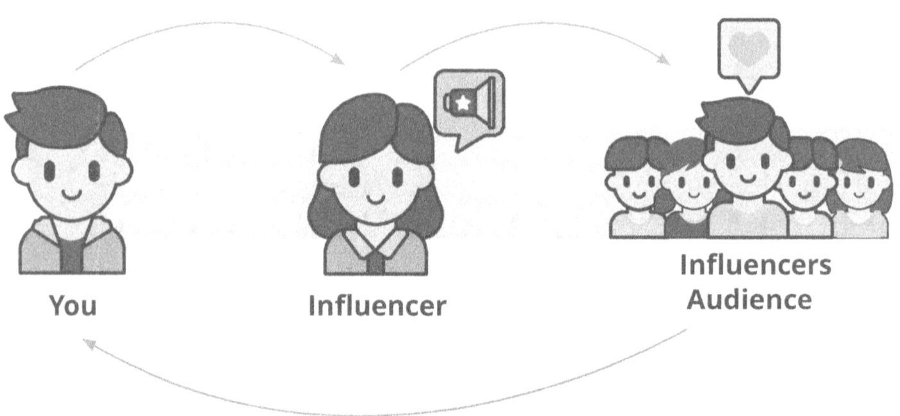

Figure 4. Influencer Trust Exchange

Authority and Expertise

Humans are trained from an early age to accept the teaching of authority. When listening to influencers, we naturally assume that they have expert knowledge, and we naturally accept opinions as factual. Influencers can market products and themselves because they are taken as an authority in the consumer's eyes. When an influencer is creating content about current trends, it just validates them as an authority.

Halo Effect

The authority of influencers within one area can easily spill into another entirely different area. When an audience trusts an influencer, that influencer can start a conversation in a new field and retain the trust of their audience.

Information Overload

Even though the Internet is a vast space filled with endless information chatter, most users rely on few sources to make decisions. In decision making, people will use cognitive biases to make what they consider proper decisions. Influencers can bypass natural human filtering of information, and in that way, they can influence a person's decision.

Social Distance

People will take the relatable influencers of closer social proximity as a more serious source of information than more prominent celebrities. This means authoritative influencers are more relatable than superstars or other celebrities.

Social Proof

People will assume a fact is right if other people already made the same assumption. Influencers with a bigger audience will give the impression of trust and expertise because other people are already confirming their expertise by engaging with their content. The same concept also solves the audience's need for belonging.

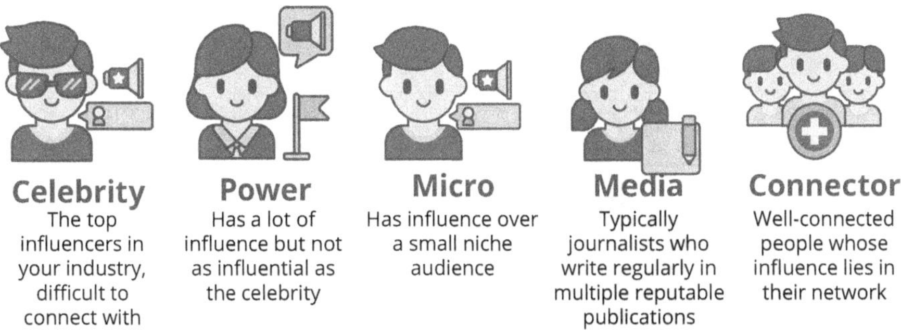

Figure 5. Influencer types in every industry

The concept of "Consumer Tribes" is introduced by Seth Godin, which places a psychological concept into marketing. Consumer tribes form when people align with a leader or idea. When people share the same values as the leader, they will follow their online presence. By following the leader's advice, consumers are trying to confirm their identity of belonging to the group.

The brain rewards social conformity and will try to prevent a decision to break with social convention. Conformity is a powerful social mechanism that we can use to participate in networks and conversation while changing how the world perceives us.

Cognitive Biases

Cognitive biases are ways of perceiving the world that may not necessarily reflect reality. Each of us sees the world based on our preconceptions, social factors, and past experiences. We can say that cognitive biases are the distortions of reality by which we view the world. Cognitive biases make us avoid uncomfortable information and stay with information that we are comfortable with.

Cognitive biases occur simply cause the brain is trying to simplify information processing in order to achieve faster decisions.

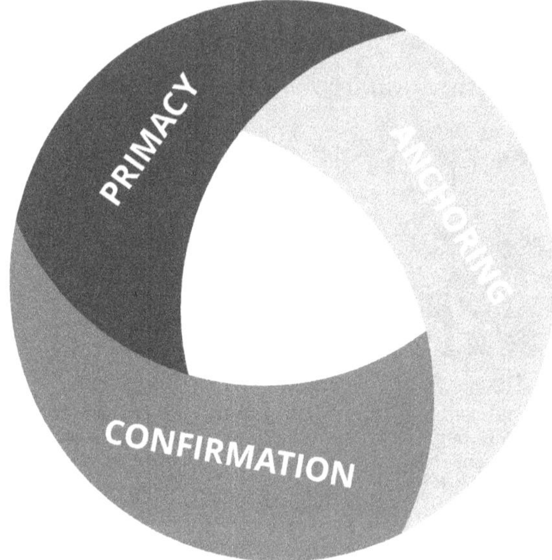

Figure 6. Cognitive biases

Three cognitive biases determine the first impressions we create about the people we see online:

* **Primacy** – We believe the first thing we hear about someone.
* **Anchoring** – After we created the first impression, it becomes hard to change our mind, which is why the first impression is hard to change.
* **Confirmation** – If you created the first impression, then the next interaction that is equally consistent with the first impression will confirm your belief. If you have a poor online

presence lacking interaction, it will confirm bad expectations. Because of confirmation bias, you need to have a virtual impression confirming real-life impressions.

There is a powerful principle of influence rooted into human psychology, called "reciprocity". People feel obliged to give back after someone does something for them. In the online world of social media, if you engage with someone's content, they will tend to return you a favor in the same way.

DIFFERENCE BETWEEN CHARACTER, BRAND, AND REPUTATION

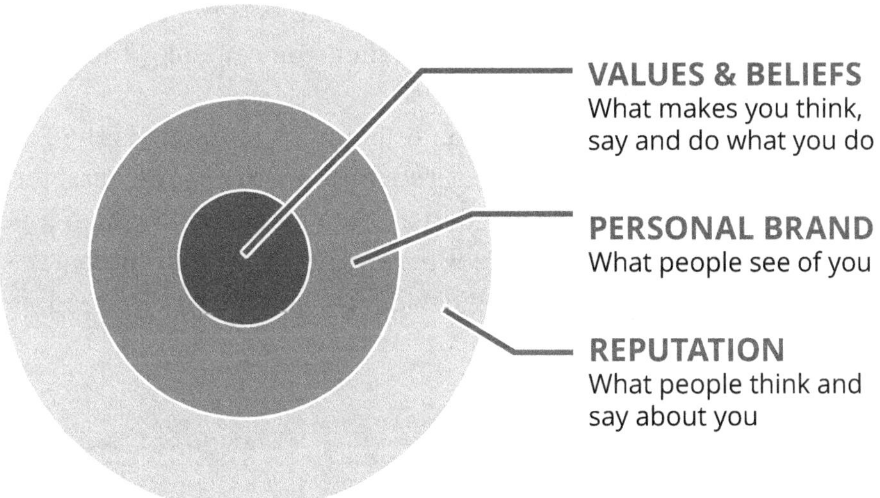

Figure 7. The difference between Character, Brand, and Reputation. Adapted from Rob Brown, 2010, p.58.

Character is defined as the distinct moral qualities of an individual. It depicts the internal characteristics of a person, which means that characteristics are under a person's control.

Reputation is defined as the subjective beliefs or opinions that are generally held about someone by others.

Reputation is an outward expression of your character. Character is the foundation of your reputation. Both of them are a necessary for a positive online reputation.

Reputation is the single greatest asset you have. Not your job title; what is really important is the projects you worked on, how much people trust you, who knows you and who you know, and the impression that you leave on people around you. No matter your current profession and line of work, you are a brand with a reputation that shouldn't be left to others to control for you. Reputation is a measurement of public opinion.

When a person tries to build a good reputation on a bad character, it cannot be sustained for a long time because reality will surface sooner or later. The best way to create lasting change in your online reputation is to do good work and form good relationships with the people around you. The better and stronger the person's real character is, the easier it is to work on reputation. When character and reputation are aligned and working together, you can enjoy the many benefits of a positive online reputation.

Most people think that reputation in personal branding is the key to success, while the reality is that reputation is built on character. Therefore, reputation is only as good as the character on which it is built. Personal branding is the tool to convert your natural characteristics into something communicable that audiences can read as reputation.

PERSONALITY'S ROLE IN PERSONAL BRANDING

People like people who are real, and more so they love the ones that allow themselves to be human – the same as any one of us.

A great personal brand must be built on your real personality, including all your traits and flaws. Behind every successful personal brand is a real person and not a fake public-relation-created personality. For your personal brand, it's best to avoid trying to create a perfect image.

A well-established personal brand will fill other people's psychological needs for leadership, creativity, service, or business behavior.

Next to professional behavior, a personal brand needs to be as human and relatable as possible.

Any personal brand has a unique style when using their skills and living their life. Personality, principles, and philosophies drive that style.

Key personality traits of a well-developed personal brand are:

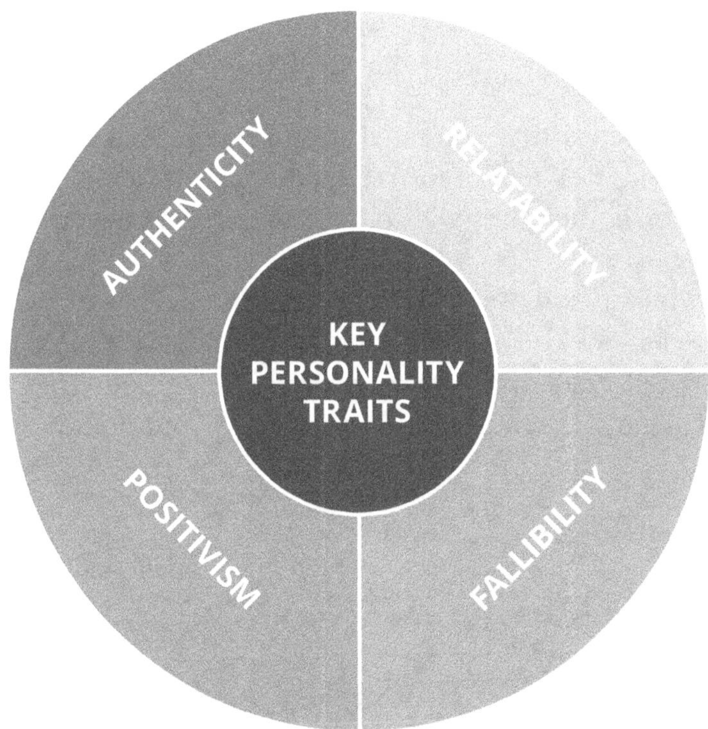

Figure 8. Key personality traits

Relatability

It allows others to identify with you, the personal brand owner, on an emotional, moral, or intellectual basis. When people recognize relatability, it will transform into a connection with the personal brand.

Fallibility

A well-developed personal brand doesn't advertise its flaws, but it does not hide them because it allows relatability. Pointing out your own flaws can be a very good thing.

Positivism

Building enthusiasm into a personal brand creates the perception of being able to persevere against all the bad odds and always finding a way to get things done. Any type of displaying negative thinking is detrimental to a personal brand. At the same time, realism combined with an action plan is a good thing.

Authenticity

Authenticity means that you need to include your real self in your personal brand. It is a base for relatability and fallibility. A personal brand built on authenticity will connect with the audience.

The Four Elements of (Building a) Personal Brand

The main elements of building a personal brand are personal credentials, social credentials, network, and recognition. They are the minimum essential parts necessary to develop your brand.

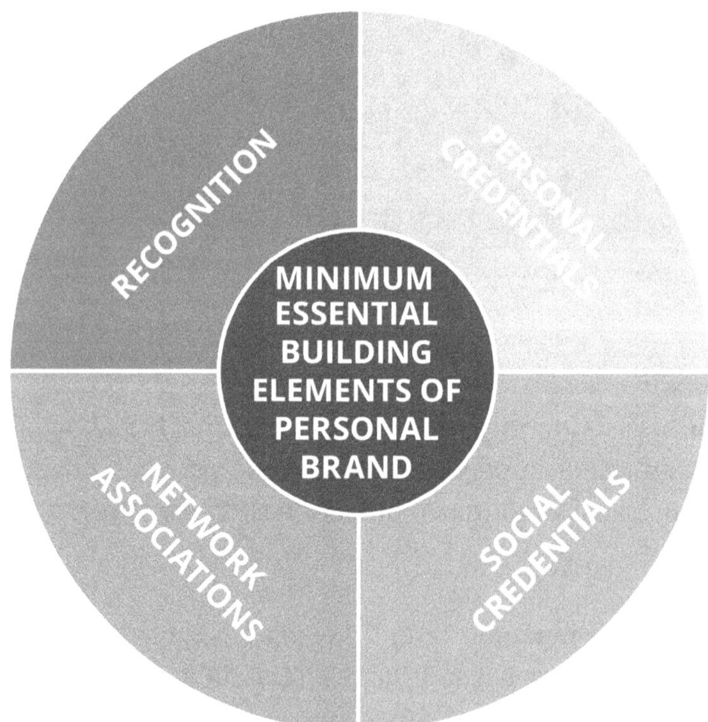

Figure 9. Minimum essential building elements of personal brand

Personal Credentials

The credentials that you earned throughout your life give you the confidence to pursue goals. They are education, experience, and achievements. Many of the people around you, even though they successfully finished and gained degrees in specific fields, are never asked to prove that they actually have a diploma. A large majority of them also do not work in the field corresponding to the diploma they possess. Personal credentials in education serve to prove that individuals are capable of finishing degrees. Whatever your personal credentials are, they will give you the confidence to create content, reach others, and communicate your value to the community.

Social Credentials

Other people will believe that you are qualified to do something by social credentials. Based on them, people will believe that they can learn something from you or that you can help them in some way. Social credentials are references and referrals, social media followers, publications, and years of experience. Usually, people like to communicate with the people of their perceived level. Simultaneously, social credentials in some fields enable you to communicate with whoever you wish in another field. An example is that a significant social following will allow you to communicate with anyone you want outside of your community because your social credentials are high.

Network Associations

The most important element of your personal brand is network association. People decide if you are what you say you are based on your network associations and your expertise. Network associations are people and companies you have worked with, your social media friends, the companies you worked for, professional organizations, and non-profits which you are a member of. Associations within networks in the digital age are very serious because who you are connected to on social media is one of the keys to building your digital personal brand. Therefore, it is essential to strategically make social media connections and then communicate your connections to the rest of the community.

Recognition

Recognition for you, as an expert in your field or at certain types of tasks, is a crucial part of your personal brand. Types of recognition are an employee of the month, top of the class, academic rewards, international rewards, any type of reward recognizing you as the best in a certain type of task.

Recognition tends to be reciprocal, which means that if you recognize someone else's efforts, they will feel obliged to do the same for you. In the digital world, collaborating on content with your friends and followers is a powerful way of recognizing. To get recognition takes time together with perseverance.

POSITIVELY EXPLAINING FLAWS

Sometimes our flaws come out, and then we can handle them positively using the following methods:

1. **Admission** – Admit the problem that you had at a particular moment (impatience, ego, other).
2. **Humor** – Apply humor to the admission of your problem and allow others to make fun of your flaw.
3. **Benefit** – Try using humor to point out your flaw as a beneficial contribution.
4. **Timing** – Always address your flaws in real-time. Otherwise, they will prevent your personal brand development or even worse come out when your brand is already developed, which will cause damage to it.

After using some of the above methods to explain your flaws positively, it is essential to control yourself in the future by working on removing your flaws.

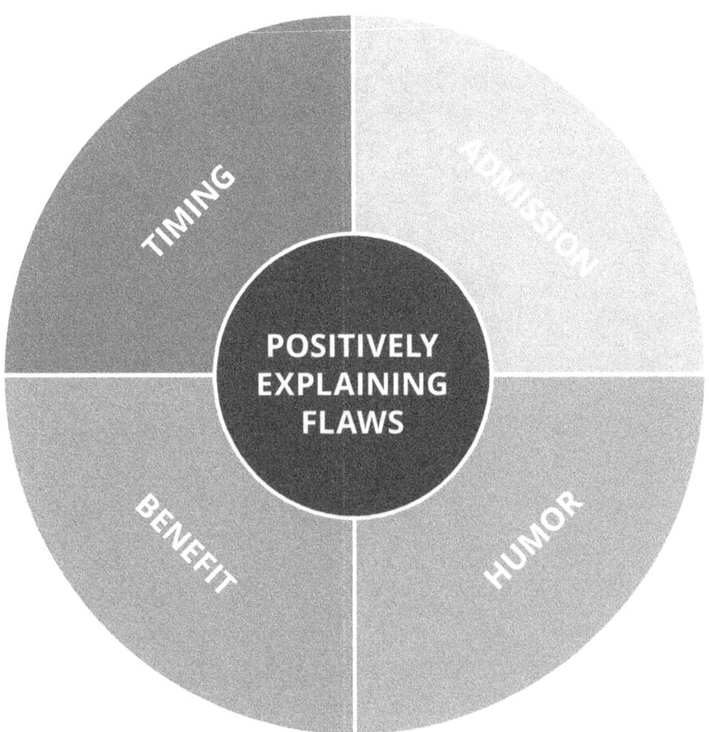

Figure 10. Positively explaining flaws

CHAPTER 3.

THE POWER OF STORYTELLING FOR PERSONAL BRANDING

If you don't give the market the story to talk about, they'll define your brand's story for you.

David Brier

SUCCESS THROUGH STORYTELLING

Digital personal Branding is an evolution of a resume. Based on our online profiles, people estimate if we are worthy of getting new opportunities. From the time of LinkedIn's formation in the year 2000, our resumes went online. Now we have websites on which we can search for anyone. Personal branding online is writing the summary of your life. We can and should be the narrators of our digital story.

In a networked online world, asking for help functions differently than in the real-life world. Even if you don't interact with someone regularly, you can reach out to them when an opportunity arises in an online environment. Simply because you have knowledge of their online presence, and they have knowledge of your online presence, including your work and values – essentially your digital personal brand.

A big part of successful content creation in online marketing is creating stories and building your brand through stories. Everyone has a story online, the only difference is that some people control their story and some do not.

A personal brand story is a narrative that follows the facts and feelings that your personal brand creates. Unlike traditional advertising, which involves showing and telling people about your brand, a story must inspire an emotional reaction.

The worst principle that can be applied online is to, through marketing efforts, convince customers that you are a hero. Such methods will have no results online and will push people away from your content and eventually prevent them from becoming your follower.

When in traditional marketing, a business hires a marketing agency, they often do not understand that product messages need to be simplified into a great story. Instead of simplifying messages, agencies tend to create more complex stories to justify their existence and fees.

Stories give form to complex situations or create in the readers a desire to engage with your content. Stories get people interested and involved.

In the real world, words convince and engage much more than the fancy design of web pages on which they are displayed.

Without simplifying and clarifying your message to distinguish yourself from others, marketing is a waste of money. It will be impossible to differentiate yourself from a competitor that merely communicates better.

No one is able to create your personal brand story better than you can. Your brand story needs to be the best it can possibly be, so that you will be the first choice of people searching online for your type of expertise. As people and their goals change over time, you naturally need to update your story.

Storytelling is an effective tool for personal branding because:

* **Persona alignment** – You can align your different personas (public, private, social) together by projecting some narrative through the story of you and your work.
* **Values conveyed** – Storytelling conveys the values that motivate and drive you, and the process humanizes you in front of the audience.
* **Trust built** – By creating a story of why you do what you do with consinstency online, it will build trust with the audience.

The only real reason people follow anyone online or engage with their content is because they expect them to provide useful, life-enhancing knowledge.

That is because all humans have a simple goal in life; they all desire to be taken somewhere. To a better life, to a brighter future, or to participate in some movement bigger than just one person.

If you define how prospects' lives and experiences will be better if they connect with you, they will want to become connected.

Digital and social media allow you to tell stories on a large scale. People are not so focused on the company brand. Instead, they are more interested in hearing the stories of the real people behind the brand.

Finding out what your audience likes to listen to and continually evalutaing and adapting to audience needs is one of the keys to success in digital and social media marketing.

Telling powerfully transformational stories about life-changing enlightenment is an excellent way to start. It is one of the types of stories that will always get the audience interested.

Speaking about people's problems will increase your personal brand connection, which works much better than running slogans about how you are more clever than anyone else.

Human beings are always searching for ways to improve their lives and to find ways that will help them survive. So, create such a story that benefits your audience instead of speaking only about your achievements and events.

In crafting product messages, a sure win is to focus on the part of human psychology that causes people to search for ways to live better, survive, and feel better (their primal needs, or Maslow's Hierarchy of Needs). Speaking about your own personal achievements does not help the customer with their primal needs. No one listens to speeches "about me".

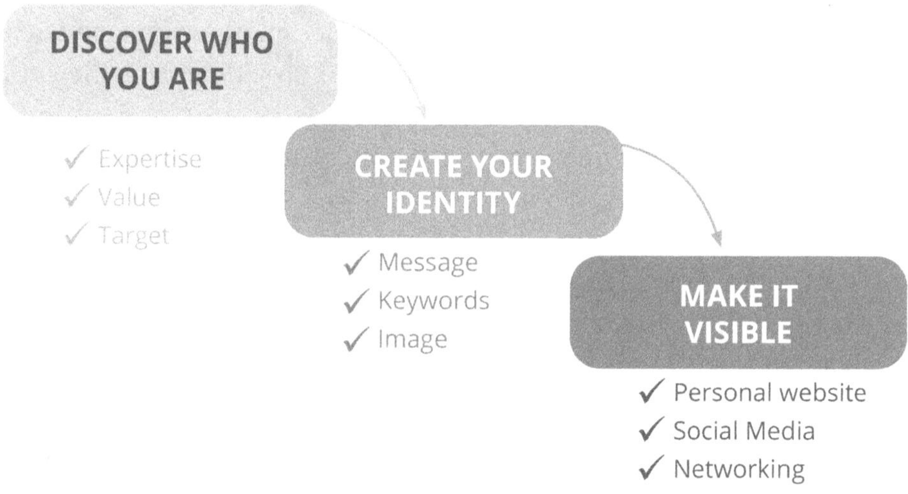

Figure 11. Process of digital personal branding

Our personal digital story is the core of authentic us, based on three components:

* **History story** – All that brought you to this moment
* **Present story** – This is the story you are living in this moment
* **Future story** – What you can achieve in the future

Any attempt to make branding efforts without putting authenticity behind it will fail when encountering the real world.

At its core, the story conveys purpose and meaning, so use storytelling to resonate with the rest of the world.

Personal Branding Keywords

Telling the search engines which words to associate with you is a constant task in digital personal branding. Keywords are not only visually important but a crucial part of Search Engine Optimization (SEO).

Therefore you need to create a list of keywords that you will use on any possible occasion when writing text, describing your personal brand or publishing social media posts. The best method is to define your personal brand with a few words and having a tagline to bring you visibility and better awareness.

You need to associate your personal brand with keywords that will be based on your expertise so that web users searching for experts in your niche can find you. Google yourself often to understand if you are making progress and see the keywords that Google associates with your personal brand.

Chosen keywords need to be applied to all social media channels that you use, and that will result in:

* The networks' search algorithms will be able to suggest you to other members
* People will scan your profile, and visually attractive keywords will convert them into followers
* Members of the network will be able to find you when they perform a network search

Choosing Personal Brand Keywords

Keyword selection will either make you visible or render you invisible, as it is the first step in SEO that determines if you are or are not easily found on any type of search engine.

How to figure out keywords:

1. Think of keywords based on what you currently do or on what you aspire to do and become in your life and career.
2. Find websites and social media sites of experts in the area you want to be known, and use their ideas and keywords as inspiration for yourself.
3. Check LinkedIn for other professionals and analyze their taglines and keywords.
4. Check job boards for job description keywords based on what you want to be or do in life.
5. Use social listening by joining niche forums to see what the audience writes and thinks about.
6. Use search tools specialized in finding keywords such as Keywordtool.io, Google Ads, Google Trends, and others.

You need to put the keywords you choose, and your tagline, wherever it makes sense to use them: on the home page and about section of your website; in any article that you write; in all the social profiles you own; and anywhere else you find a place for them.

Spend time thinking about keywords because to have a successful digital personal brand you need to consider what people type into search engines.

CRAFTING YOUR PERSONAL BRAND STORY

After meeting you for the first time, people will remember you by one or two things. You can and should decide what that will be.

If you try to be too many things simultaneously, people will not even remember what you do or why they should ever contact you.

To get your story clear, you need to decide on a differentiated value you bring and a precise category in which you want to be known.

Every effective personal brand starts with positioning yourself in the competitive environment to begin to differentiate yourself. Career goals are the basis of your positioning because they will help you make crucial choices regarding your personal brand.

Positioning will create the basis for developing all your critical messages for a variety of audiences.

When you are able to craft your story compellingly, your message will be liked by the audience. Your story should clarify your positioning while also providing pieces of evidence for all the claims of your personal brand.

When positioning yourself, then you use the following model to craft a statement:

* Who's your target audience?
* What's their Issue?
* From which field are you (your category)?
* What's your value proposition?
* What differentiates you from the competition?

In the above statement, you are the product that your audience desires.

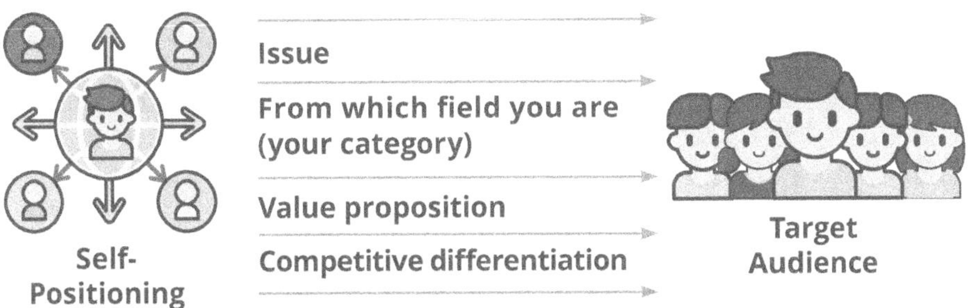

Figure 12. Statement of self-positioning for effective diferentiation

Deciding on your target audience depends on your goals. For example, if you want to change jobs, then your target audience is either management of your desired company or their human resources personel.

When defining a problem statement, you need to position yourself as a solution. So you need to think about what you can have as an offer to solve issues that your audience might have. That creates your value proposition.

You also need to distinguish yourself between other people that have the same desire as you do. This is where your expertise comes in. By sharing knowledge from your expertise, you create value.

If you cannot support providing values because you simply lack skills, you will have to solve that issue and acquire skills. Joining groups of experts, volunteering, teaching for free, or helping the community will allow you to support your claims about value by providing real context.

Positioning will give you an idea of your value and differentiate you from others.

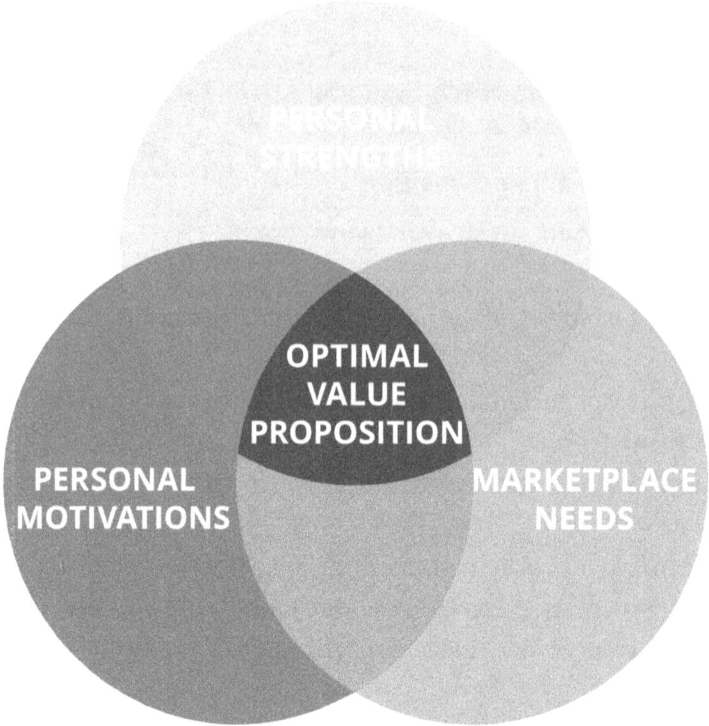

Figure 13. Personal value proposition

Your personal brand basic story needs to be formulated using the following guide:

* What I do/or desire to do
* Context of the value that you bring
* Evidence of your claims

When you address different audiences, your value message will naturally be different because their issues differ.

When communicating to an audience about the topic, you craft your message as:

* What audience desires
* What is the challenge to achieve those desires
* Value message about the topic

Whenever you make claims, you need to provide proof in order to make them credible.

Creating a tagline for yourself about what you do, for example, "Electric Car Enthusiast and Visionary", is essential for people to understand you. You will be using it all over the social media profile setup and anywhere else online .

Categories of content that will help you build and place your story online are:

* **Achievements –** Creating a sentence for each of your achievements while aspiring in the same sentence to a new goal in life.

* **Values –** Create a sentence for each of your values, but limiting it to only important ones will help distinguish your personal brand.

* **Abilities –** Create a sentence about your main strengths in terms of what you think you can do with more quality than anyone else.

* **Differentiation –** Create a sentence about what is different in your work, personality, and educational background that could bring value.

* **Facts –** Quantify your claims by providing exact numbers on how you brought value.

* **Evidence –** Name awards, colleagues' recommendations, endorsements or testimonials, memberships in society or interest groups, or media where your articles were published or you were quoted.

The above mentioned categories are all that you need to be able to craft your personal brand story.

STORYTELLING FOR CONTENT CREATION

The content you offer tells the world your principles and values that you uphold and how you bring value to the world. It demonstrates you professionally.

A *thought leader* is a person that the public trusts within a certain niche. What is visible immediately is that thought leaders are also fantastic content creators.

Content marketing is publishing valuable content to attract and engage an audience.

The effects of great content are:
* Attracting audiences
* Engaging audiences
* Displaying your skills and knowledge
* Growing your reach
* Increasing your social media presence

To be successful at digital story telling it is needed to think in a way of combining different elements of content planning and distribution that will together create a great story and effective story telling. Elements of successful digital story telling are shown in Figure 14.

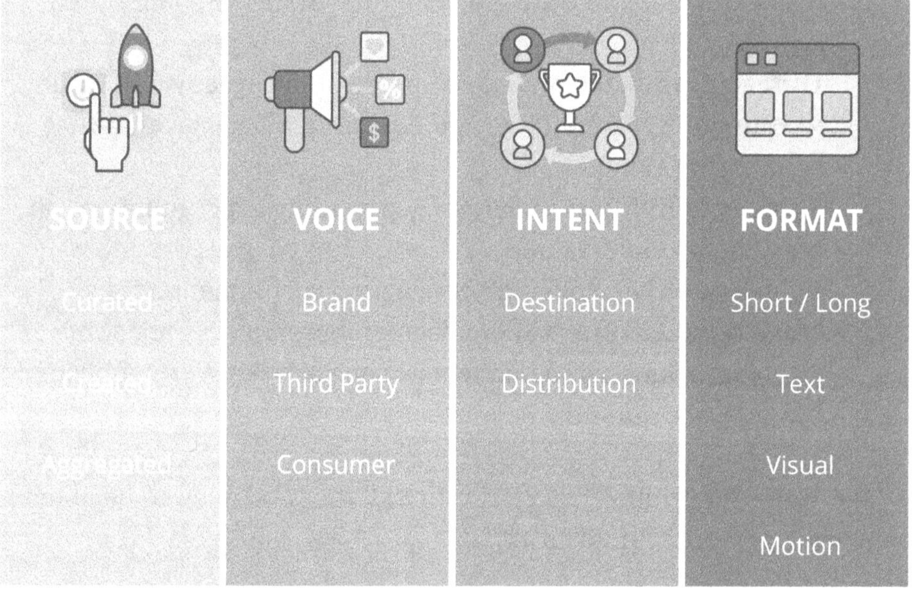

Figure 14. Elements of successful digital story telling

Creating stories is the most powerful tool in organizing complex information into something useful so that audiences will want to hear it.

People will always gladly walk into a story that helps them to achieve more in life or become more. The story should be simple and clear.

A good story can hold our focus for hours, and a story is the best way to fight through the information noise that most humans are bombarded with every second of their life. The typical error is that brands speak about themselves.

People will relate to situations and events that they understand more often than listening to a very wealthy celebrity influencer's message.

To make a message in your content story simple and clear, use the following questions when crafting it:

1. What do members of the audience desire?
2. What do the audience members not desire, or what blocks them from their desires?
3. How lost will the members of the audience feel if they do not get their desires?

If those three questions are not answered in your message, the audience gets lost in too many similar words and will search for other online solutions.

Any part of the story that doesn't explain these three fundamental issues needs to be removed. All elements that do not serve the story need to go.

Then just formulate the story even better by using this pattern of questions:

1. What advice do you offer that they can relate to?
2. How does your advice make customers' lives better?

THE SECRETS OF A GREAT STORY

The main character of your personal brand story is your future follower, who always searches for ways that can help them to achieve what they want in life. By addressing issues that prevent your future followers from pursuing happiness faster, you will gain their attention.

The leading cause of frustration to any person is the one single enemy causing it, even if there are many contributing factors. So, it's best to define the single enemy and make it relatable and real.

So you need to clarify to your audience what their enemy is in the story you are telling them and that your personal brand can offer them help.

People are online looking for a guide in life who will help them, not another main character of their story. So, anyone who positions themselves as the main character in other people's stories will fail to gain their attention. People should always be the main character of their own stories.

Humans focus on primitive survival instincts: food, warmth, happiness, having children. We can relate that to the modern way of life as having money, building social networks, and buying luxury items.

Being associated with authority in some field belongs to one of the primal human instincts: being associated with power, which can help humans survive.

The desire for meaning is one of the most influential motivators, as life becomes intolerable without a purpose. Therefore, craft a message that will invite the people to participate in something bigger than just reading your message, invite them to be in your community, and actively participate in the conversation.

Everyone is looking for a guide in life, and when you try to position yourself as something else than a guide, then you are destined to fail with your communication.

To make people follow us, we need to tell them where we are taking them.

Your personal brand in online communication needs to focus on three levels of a problem (frustration) that exist for the audience in their lives: internal, external, and philosophical.

Philosophical problems are defined as a more substantial, more in-depth story for a customer than our brand is on a mission to solve. For example, good must prevail over evil.

People are searching for a solution for their internal problems, which would help them become successful in life and solve external problems that disrupt their experience of life.

Framing your solutions to address internal, external, and possibly philosophical problems immediately increases your brand's value in the audience's eyes.

CHAPTER 4.

WRITING LIKE AN EFFICIENT WRITER

If your content isn't driving conversation, you're doing it wrong.

Dan Roth

Efficient Writing

Compelling content is relevant and useful to your readers. Your writing should speak in the language of a reader, on a reader level, and discuss problems that they have.

To make people read your content, it has to be helpful and useful. Only then will people connect with you. When you show your expertise to people, positioning yourself as a guide, then they will start to trust you. That relationship where you are guiding the reader to the solution of their problem will create great trust.

Traditional media communicates using "one-to-many" platforms, conversely online communication is "many-to-many." People's increased trust in peer-to-peer communication minimizes the influence of traditional advertising. A major sin today in marketing is a lack of relevance.

The new reality of marketing online is that it's the public, instead of marketing departments, which creates marketing messages. In engaging audiences online over the long term, it will not be clear where marketing ends and selling starts. In a connected world where people have numerous channels for communication, the most crucial channel is word-of-mouth.

Making that content available where people can find it is the next step to positioning. Develop a keyword strategy to target keywords that people enter in search engines. Seek "long-tail keywords" in the form of three words or longer phrases, and include them in your communications. Also, make sure your content is worthy of sharing. There is nothing more effective than people sharing your content on their social network sites.

Figure 15. The Writing Process

ENGAGING WITH EFFICIENT CONTENT

When you analyze successful online content, you will notice a pattern in the types of content that are usually more popular than the average: They're created based on satisfying human psychology.

There are approximately twenty-one themes of content that all humans crave and they like to read and engage with online. Content that:

1. Reminds us life is short
2. Reminds us dreams can come true

3. Gives us faith to believe in bigger things
4. Reminds us that we matter
5. Reminds us of the overlooked or forgotten "basics"
6. Has unexpected twists
7. Tells us a story
8. Takes us along on a journey
9. Inspires us to action
10. Makes us laugh or smile
11. Makes us cry (tears of joy or sadness)
12. Reveals secrets
13. Surprises us
14. Encourages us never to give up
15. Reminds us that we are one of a kind and encourages us to live that way
16. Reminds us that there is more to life than trivial things
17. Confirms our assumptions
18. Challenges our assumptions
19. Educates us while entertaining us
20. Involves David defeating Goliath
21. Gives us a fresh point of view even about everyday things

Formulating your content based on the themes mentioned above will, for sure, create content that appeals to your readers.

At *www.dariosipos.com/resources* you can download a helpful infographic, "Types of Content That All Humans Crave".

Additionally, applying the below elements to your writing, will add to your content success:

* Using an attention-grabbing headline
* Writing in a tone relevant to readers
* Including content that helps the reader to understand a topic better
* Adding to the conversation instead of recycling content that exists
* Writing content in a way that people perform a search
* Building a structure (use subheadings)

* Choosing one central idea of writing
* Supporting your brand message, value, and strategy
* Inserting a call to action
* Checking for grammatical errors

When you write, cut out anything that does not support your main idea while writing in simple language using an active voice. Be clear and concise.

Write for a specific platform, making sure that your tone of voice and way of writing fit the platform for which you are writing. Use short sentences and paragraphs. Remove extra words or corporate jargon. Be even more conversational by using "you" and "your" to connect directly with the reader.

WRITING POWERFUL HEADLINES

A catchy headline is your opportunity to gain the casual browser and convert them to an avid reader. Based on some studies done by Nielsen Norman Group, around 80% of visitors, when reading longer posts, will read a headline but only 20% will actually finish reading it.

Headlines can be post headlines, headlines of articles, or headlines of product listings on your e-commerce site. Bad headlines will cause your content marketing to fail.

Steps to writing powerful headlines:

1. Use specific numbers and data
2. Use underlying reason
3. Call for attention
4. Use headline formulas

Usually, search engines ignore characters beyond the sixty-second, so keep your headlines short to avoid them being clipped.

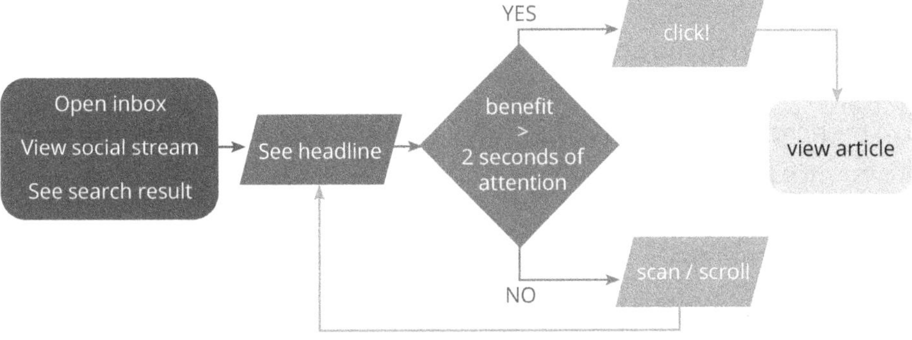

Figure 16. How readers process your headlines. Adapted from Orbitmedia.

Use Specific Numbers and Data

Headlines create around 52% of the effectiveness of your posts. Research shows that headlines containing numbers can generate up to 70% more engagement. Odd numbers in the headline will have more success than even numbers in about 20% of cases.

When writing headlines, use numerals instead of words for numbers, because that too is a successful step to better engagement and a shorter, more straightforward headline.

If you are creating guides for your audience for any field, then never use more than nine steps.

Use Underlying Reason

In a headline, use the underlying reason why some action should be done, giving people a good reason to read your content.

The best words to include in your headlines are: Reasons, Lessons, Ideas, Tips, Tricks, Facts, Secrets, Strategies.

Some examples:

5 Reasons Why Having a New Phone Is a Must

9 Facts About Your Phone That You Didn't know

3 Secrets to Buying a Cheap TV

Call for Attention

The headline should make the viewer read the first sentence and call for attention because attention spans are on average just eight seconds. There is no such thing as excellent content without a captivating headline that will grab the reader's attention.

The headline can convince your readers to continue reading your posts until the end.

Any successful headline should apply these four rules:
* Communicate that the subject is useful
* Include urgency in it
* Make it unique
* Be very specific

Use Headline Formulas

As you create your content, you will discover formulas for headlines that work for you. Usually, content is created before writing a headline because you will be able to match the headline much better with the text after it is written.

One of the formulas, for example, is to identify the problem, offer a solution, make a promise the solution will work.

A headline is an integral part of your content no matter the format, but when writing longer posts, the introduction, subtitles, bullet points, and call to action are equally important.

The best approach is to use storytelling (story branding) and data-driven content to build your authority, all while solving the reader's problems.

CATCHING ATTENTION IN UNDER SIX SECONDS

The attention span of humans is now on average shorter than ever before – about eight seconds.

Getting hold of people's attention is a dicey game of hit and miss; with the vast deluge of information permeating our cyberspace every single minute, it is hard to keep focus on what is important.

If you're a content publisher looking to grab scarce attention, here are five strategies to consider:

* Make it simple, concise, and relatable
* Master content delivery channels
* Include video
* Take the direct approach
* Include interactive content

Simple, Concise, and Relatable

People hate what they find hard to understand. If you are going to catch them and keep them hooked, then whatever information you are presenting must be easy to understand and easy to relate with, especially in the first instance. An excellent way to do this is to introduce what you are trying to present by piggybacking it on a familiar concept.

Mastering Content Delivery Channels

Every digital platform – the media through which most content gets to end-users – has its own peculiar set of written and unwritten rules. When you know these rules (and all the blind spots), it becomes easier to present your information in the manner that appeals best to your target demographic. The more audience-specific or tailored your content is, the more engaging it will turn out to be.

Of course, these rules vary across the board for different digital platforms. Twitter, for instance, is the revered home for short and spicy bursts of information, so naturally, you will want to keep it toned down on there. Audiences on LinkedIn – a site for professionals – will, on the other hand, prefer detailed expositions on any subject matter.

Including Video

If you have been a publisher for long enough, then you have probably come across the popular "video is everything" school of thought – every major digital platform is moving towards video, and you should too. Well, not quite. While video does remain a high impact content distribution format, it is not a magic wand to fix all your engagement and conversion problems.

If you push bland unoptimized content through video, it will change very little. Worse still, it can actually hurt your current engagement.

What you can do with video, however, is to present otherwise bland content in a captivating way. "Captivating" can be very subjective, but some evergreen strategies include, spicing it up with humor, artistry, controversy, or, better still, all three.

Taking the Direct Approach
Sometimes all your audience needs to keep up with you is an answer to the question "why should I listen to you?" And sometimes, the perfect answer to this question is a simple truth. You have probably, at one point, come across fishy articles, videos, or ads with what we like to call "clickbait" titles. Something along the lines of:

This Man Shares the Secret to Making Millions from Home

How to Succeed in an Office Environment

This Is Exactly How Algorithms Work

These titles will get clicks because they provide direct answers to questions many people have on their minds. You, too, can grab the attention of your audience by giving straightforward answers to the questions that are on their minds.

Interactive Content
The Internet is very one-dimensional. Everyone is pushing tons of content to internet users, and no one bothers about their side of the story. As an internet user myself, trust me when I say it can get exhaustive and not to mention boring.

Making content interactive will prevent it from being dull and exhausting.

When content is presented as a two-way street, one where a publisher releases content and the input of the audience is sought and appreciated, then the user feels the need to interact with the publisher. So, when the users want to interact with you as a publisher then, congratulations, you have successfully captured their attention.

The best part? It is not just for eight seconds – you get to decide how long you want to keep them hooked.

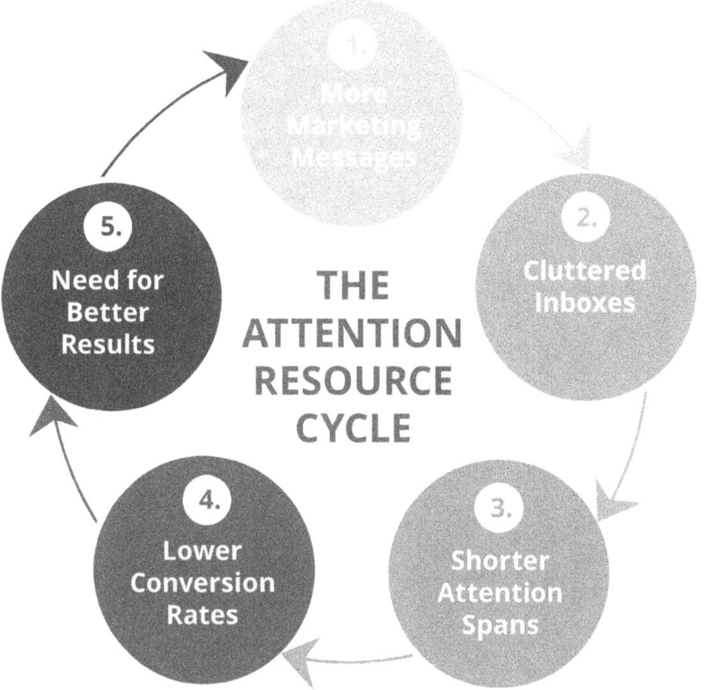

Figure 17. Attention resource cycle

CHAPTER 5.

GOALS WITH PERSONAL DIGITAL BRANDING

Brand yourself for the career you want, not the job you have.

Dan Schawbel

I N THIS CHAPTER, WE WILL speak about branding based on groups of people of similar characteristics. The mentioned groups of people are similar by their goals, experience, values, and their current life situation. By creating these groups, we can address each group's most common issues and provide a view on bigger goals, such as relocating abroad or working internationally as an expert in your field.

Most people who will decide on your job application, career move, business, and entrepreneurship support will search for you online before you sit in front of them at the meeting.

If you contact them online, they will then research your personal profile online; therefore, providing to them a personal layout brand online is necessary to progress in your desired direction.

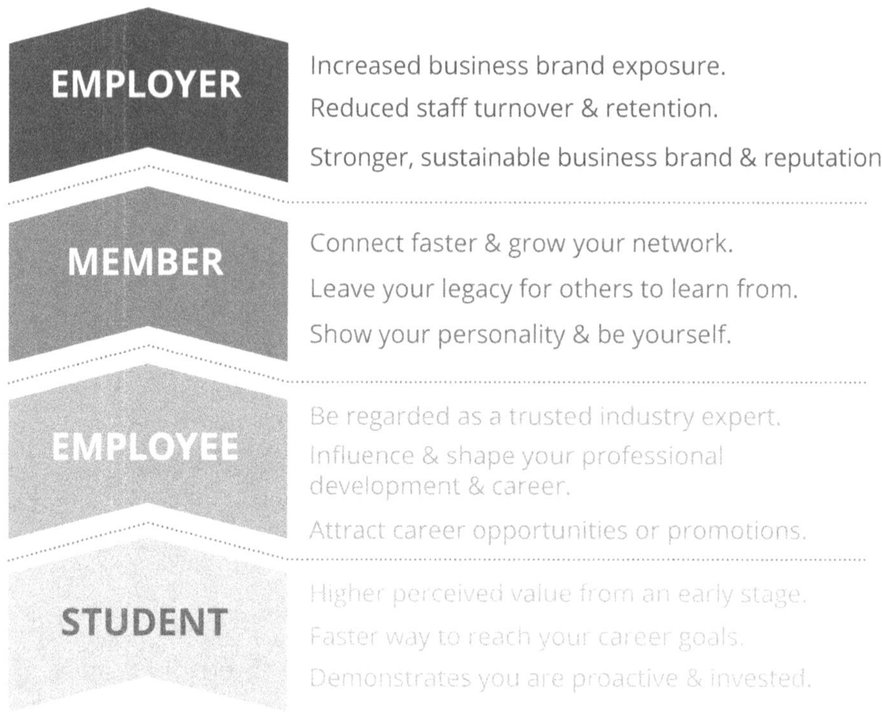

Figure 18. Personal branding benefits everyone

Young Professionals

Most students still think that after getting a diploma, the perfect job waits around the corner, together with a long, successful, well-paid career.

Students after graduating don't only face competition with their colleagues but with the older people in the same field because online education and changing qualifications became popular even for the people already established in the workforce.

More than ever, students who just entered the workforce need to differentiate themselves and stand out. Here, digital personal branding comes into play because it is quite hard to stand out before starting work.

Most real-world experiences can be collected via volunteering, internships, and doing projects for free.

What can distinguish a student from another in a digital personal brand is, for example, projects, internships, foreign languages, and belonging to networks and groups. Showing these experiences and interests while also participating in online conversations confirms their job aspirations.

At the start of their career, a young professional works on gaining experience during a period of establishing themselves and their future career goals. To increase their personal brand, they need to build their networks by offering help to others and expanding their communication skills through networking and social media communication.

Updating their online profiles with the newest information on accomplishments and newly gained workplace skills is essential. Expanding expertise, by taking online courses and providing free help to others based on a newly acquired skill set, will help to establish them as an authority and give them material for content marketing – and further develop them as a person.

Taking a leadership role in any project makes the personal brand more visible when some content is created around the profile. LinkedIn has feature "projects" where it is possible to mark who was project leader together with mentioning all the project team members.

Online, students can present their ideas to improve some local or business issues in general because that will boost visibility.

What personal branding online does is keep people looking fresh in their career choice and enable them to grow in the direction they set. Online, anyone can set up their aspirations and continually evolve their personal brand.

To energize your career, find the expertise you like. If you are not already a top expert, learn all that you can on that subject to become a leading expert. Then create communication around that expertise online and you will become known in the field.

Keeping your personal brand updated and spiced up with new skills, projects, and expertise will keep it fresh and evolving.

EXPERIENCED PROFESSIONALS

Changing Careers

Reinventing yourself every few years is a good thing to refresh your career or establish yourself in another field. Self-reinvention doesn't mean that you need to become someone else. It is more about finding authentic pieces of yourself that you want to express and use in the real world more. Starting a new career when you are already mature is easier than you think, and digital personal branding will help you a lot.

The only obstacle to branding yourself digitally for another career is a lack of confidence. If you already have years of experience in your field working for the same company, that means you lost touch with the marketplace job search rules. Therefore you need to invest serious effort in researching new workplace rules. Suppose you consider yourself too old for a new career. In that case, you have to understand that mature workers are considered more hardworking, honest, and loyal. The only obstacle is that mature workers are usually seen as lacking new technology use, especially social media. That is where digital personal branding can help a lot and brand you as an energetic and social media enthusiast.

Suppose nobody knows about your years of experience and energy you bring into work, especially if you are trying to join a new field. In that case, you have to increase your visibility as an expert in your new field.

Communicating your personal brand value can be done by crafting your online profile and identity, connecting with groups and associations, building your network, volunteering, writing, consulting, and teaching.

Executives

Executives usually accept the personal branding concept fast because they assume that it must work for them too if it works for their company brands. To avoid being connected only with the companies they work for, executives often work on their public image more often than any other part of society. Still, it doesn't mean that all executives use digital personal branding, most likely because they struggle with the concept as they think it is unnecessary and let their work speak for itself.

Digital Personal branding of executives is a way for companies to achieve a competitive edge.

Some results from the Weber Shandwick study about building a company's reputation include:

* 73.5% believe a CEO's reputation influences employee attraction and retention
* CEOs who display authentic qualities are outranking those who do not
* 44% see the market value of the company reflected by a CEO's reputation
* CEOs are active in looking for ways to tell company stories and engage better

The strong personal brand of the executive will benefit the company in two important ways:

Increasing credibility and trust of the company – Today's consumers are very skeptical of any company, so they will do their fair share of online research before doing business with a company. Executives, such as the CEO, who have trustworthy digital personal brands help to show the company they work for in the same trustworthy light.

Company Promotional Opportunities are more effective – Executives with highly visible digital personal brands will get the opportunity to promote their companies because the media will ask them to give interviews. Suppose such an executive tries to contact publications for some PR announcement wrapped in an interview. In that case, they will be more successful than the marketing departments in pitching the same idea.

When CEOs and executives around them plan to lead the company's digital transformation, it is crucial that they lead by example of having a strong digital presence. For CEOs, we can say that they are the company brand's personification, so having a digital personal brand has become an essential aspect of their company position. CEOs and other executives are the most influential business brand ambassadors, so building their brand is on the same level of importance as building a brand for products and services the company sells.

Boundaries between internal and external communications have disappeared due to digital society; LinkedIn, for example, is an incredibly powerful platform. CEOs and executives portraying a positive image of organizations through their digital brands will motivate and attract new, qualified, quality employees.

A company with executives with a highly visible digital personal brand will be aiming higher in their competitive field, especially during challenging times in the business. When investors seek investment opportunities, they are seeking companies where CEOs have confidence and strong direction. Doing digital personal branding right will make the CEO visible in front of investors' eyes.

The most successful CEOs will digitally communicate their business goals with their voice and narrative of what is happening in their lives.

INDEPENDENT PROFESSIONALS

Digital personal branding is ideal for service professionals, such as doctors, lawyers, accountants, and any other professional that makes a living from selling expertise. Selling a service that is not a tangible product perfectly matches the digital environment and can use digital marketing channels for success.

Communicating what type of person you are together with your value proposition is essential to finding clients when you work as an independent professional. The personal brand sells the service to the client, so your personal brand must always be clearly visible online.

As an entrepreneur, your personal brand is at the center of your business. A personal brand is crucial for your business because your personal brand is intertwined with the business.

Personal branding for independent professionals fuels business growth in the way of:

Acquiring higher paying clients: When you establish a digital personal brand in your industry, your demand will increase. Therefore you can charge more for your services. Professional branding through your personal brand will help you demonstrate your value

Gaining a competitive advantage: By differentiating and positioning yourself as an authority in your field, your credibility will increase in your target market.

Deeper relationships: The digital personal brand is the most powerful sales, marketing, and networking tool that exists today. By building online relationships, it will expand your network and generate more leads and business. By interacting with your existing clients you can deepen existing relationships.

Reasons why creating your digital personal brand is good for your business if you are an independent professional or small business owner:

* **More channels for your business** – When you brand yourself as an expert in a topic or within a field, you actually build another channel through which more people can discover you.

* **Establishing authority** – When you appear digitally in different channels, such as YouTube podcasts or blog posts, you are showing people that you are more than a salesperson. You are not pitching a product, but you are an actual expert in that field. Customers prefer to buy from experts instead of salespeople.

* **Networking opportunities** – Connecting with an extensive network of people means you will meet more people you can learn from. In that way, you will get invitations to speak on events where you can grow even stronger connections outside your field.

BOOK AUTHORS (WRITERS, ARTISTS)

People will often like the author before they start reading the book. Only the author's personal branding power will reach the first readers who will decide to buy your book and give it a chance.

Branding as a book author is how the author presents their books to the public and themselves as a writer, simulatenously. It represents what people think and believe about you even before they start reading the book.

Digital personal branding is crucial if authors want to sell their books. When crafting a brand for book authors, they need to compose an identity that accurately represents who they are. At the same time, it must be compelling and relatable to the audience. Digital personal branding will help name recognition, which is necessary when the author has their next book ready for sales.

Personal branding for the authors is a mix of personal and professional branding because it includes what the author does, why they do it, and for whom.

Authors must be able to clearly communicate their vision and purpose behind their work with one single voice of importance to society. For that reason, personal branding is behind the successful development of a writer platform.

Developing a personal author brand allows authors to position themselves for the best opportunities so they can attract their ideal readers, sponsors and receive media opportunities.

By digital personal branding, authors give face and name to their writing business and become real and distinctive instead of being just another generic author.

Because people buy more on emotion than on logic, by building a community that is engaged around their messaging authors will build trust and loyalty from their readers.

Book authors were in the past branded by emphasizing the book's sales volume instead of a relationship with the readers. The new approach is to create relationships with the readers to create a community of supporters.

The book author's digital personal brand determines the level of book sales and then generates new opportunities.

The core of the marketing strategy of a book is to create and consistently present the personal author brand.

Authors shouldn't wait for people to guess about them and their work, but instead, they should tell them exactly what they want them to know.

RELOCATING ABROAD

Because your target market for which you brand yourself is specific, that means your digital personal brand developed to match your target market is not worldwide universal. People of different cultures might perceive your brand differently, so you need to adapt it to different target markets.

If you wish to work internationally, you need to create your personal branding by intertwining it with each of your target markets' specifics.

For example, after you create your digital personal brand for a country where you work, you can ask yourself if this type of communication would be accepted in another market where you would like to work.

Additionally, it is essential to study how to promote your digital personal brand in the new country. Many countries have specific sites, portals, and some even do not share the social networks that you might be using. So opening profiles on social networks specific to the country where you would like to work and making your digital personal brand visible is a great move.

Before relocating abroad, search online information about all specifics of communications in the country. Then closely examine your digital personal brand to determine what you need to change in your profiles. Find a few successful people in the country and analyze their profiles, then apply what works for them on your profiles. One of the biggest mistakes that expats make is to assume that what works in one culture will work in another.

Assertiveness, which you communicate in your online presence, might be too offensive or aggressive for another culture. Therefore you need to adjust the tone of your communication and emotions that you display in online communication.

In many countries, the company's tradition is important; therefore, they might not appreciate words like "transformation", "disruptive change," and you will have to adapt that part of your communication.

When addressing people in different cultures, you should learn the etiquette of communication in that culture.

An international digital personal brand is a great tool that will help you if you plan to live abroad. Even without looking for a job abroad, your international personal brand will help you stand out and get new opportunities locally.

For an international digital personal brand, you should highlight all the international experiences, showcase skills necessary to succeed abroad, such as language skills, and express a desire to work in an international and multicultural environment.

The set of keywords that you use in your digital profile is crucial, so you can be found by recruiters and employers who will use search engines to find job candidates.

Creating an international digital personal brand is key to being successful when searching for some opportunity abroad. At the same time, it will give you a competitive advantage over others in your local marketplace.

EMPLOYEES AS COMPANY INFLUENCERS

When companies help employees build their personal brand, it results in increased company exposure and more engaged, happier employees.

Employees as influencers is an effective way of using the people that work in a company to promote it. All research done on the subject of public trust in a company has shown that employees are trusted more than CEOs

To get employees engaged, companies need to make sure that employees feel like valued contributors to the business success.

Companies should be encouraging employees to write articles on their areas of expertise and publish them on online platforms. That way, employees will build their personal brand so that it will benefit both them personally and the company. Additionally, they should build their personal brand by sharing relevant company and industry news on social media channels.

Instead of just continuing to use traditional marketing methods, brands and companies are forced to use influencers to increase their online brand awareness. Instead of only focusing on brand ambassadors, it is far more effective to search for influencers inside companies.

Employee influencers can effect a brand's image, bringing engagement and motivating company customers and audiences to act.

Even though many companies understand the value of social media, they only rarely know how to measure it. That is the reason that many companies count on the help of employees to become influencers.

Figure 19. The benefits of having employees as company influencers

To engage employees as company influencers, management can offer employees the opportunity of promoting their personal brands alongside the company's. Companies should provide employees the content that will help them become experts in their fields. Employees are already social, so companies just need to help them have a voice that benefits them and the company. Once the company empowers employees, they will become the most active company social influencers. Behind successful social selling are the good online personal brands of the company management team and employees.

In a nutshell, social selling is marketing and sales working together online, complementing each other's efforts to listen and engage with prospects using social media networks to generate leads and execute sales.

Employee advocacy is the promotion and online support of a company by its employees. It is a fantastic way to increase company brand awareness and recognition while helping employees become thought leaders online.

Employees that promote the company online will attract other potential employees to join company ranks.

Any company's successful digital transformation starts when management has strong personal online profiles that set the new company's digital direction.

Employees are already aware that to be successful they need to be company ambassadors, even though they might only stay with the company for a few years.

CHAPTER 6

BUILDING YOUR DIGITAL PERSONAL BRAND ONLINE

Your brand isn't what you say it is, it's what Google says it is.

Chris Anderson

BUILDING DIGITAL ASSETS

Your future employees, colleagues, or anyone that you plan to meet can, at any time, search for your name online. That is the reason that you need to know what they will find when they search for you.

The online message of your personal brand needs to describe your essential professional qualities. The message should display your personal qualities, your professional characteristics, and how you apply all of that to your work.

People who claim to be experts online will be believed more than people who do not claim they are experts.

Having your brand online is similar to meeting people in person because they form an impression about you based on the first thing they see.

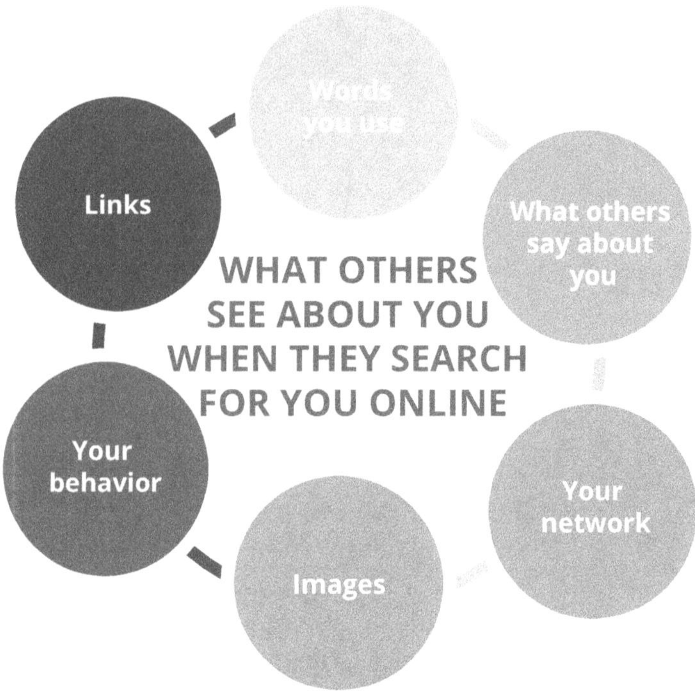

Figure 20. What others see about you when they search for you online

When people search for you online, they see the words you use, what others say about you, your network, images, your behavior, and links.

Posting, sharing, or engaging with misinformation is a colossal mistake for your personal brand.

The process of building your online presence and social media profiles can be time-consuming, difficult, and tiring, especially if you do not know how to do it.

Usually, your personal digital brand's foundation is a central online hub from which you then start building the rest of your digital resources. Typically, your central hub is your website with your own domain name (something like: *www.firstnamelastname.com*) containing your complete biography. This website or central hub can then be used as the foundation for all your social media sites.

Social media impressions will be more personal than any written communication because they will contain visual elements, including pictures and videos.

The best first step is to choose a name for your profiles, title, and a short bio that you will use throughout your social media profiles and online presence.

To quickly check over 500 sources for available names, you can use sites such as KnowEm: *www.knowem.com* or Namechk: *www.namechk.com*. KnowEm will check your brand, product, or username to search on over 575 popular social media networks so you can secure your brand across the social web. Namechk will do the same but will not search for website names available using your desired name.

Online channels on which you want to secure your name are:
* Your own website
* Medium
* LinkedIn
* Twitter
* Facebook
* Instagram
* YouTube
* Pinterest
* Quora
* SlideShare

For all the digital channels it's necessary to have a good headshot image and a short bio (up to 150 words) together with a more detailed bio.

Getting more education and specific knowledge from online classes and online events perfectly enhances your digital personal brand. Also, attending networking events and speaking with people online in your area of expertise will serve as personal proof of your activities. There are numerous such opportunities online.

Opportunities such as public speaking, networking, or participating in something bigger than yourself (for example, a membership organization) will look excellent on your profiles. Finding opportunities to speak online or at an actual event can be found on sites such as *www.speakerhub.com* and *www.speakermatch.com*.

Using rich media is essential to get your digital brand noticed. Rich media can range from pictures showing how you deliver value to complex infographics by which you display your expertise.

Personal brand pictures on digital channels are most effective when they display your professional value. Such images can:

* Present interesting situations, for example meetings with partners or colleagues
* Show you excelling at work, for example receiving a work related award
* Be you in the company of someone interesting and relevant, for example a leading expert in your industry
* Show how you are performing effectively in your career, for example speaking at an event

When you take images at events or with other people, they can tag you in pictures that will also provide social proof.

Video is a vital component of successful branding because it builds trust, differentiates you, and is popular. Videos have more chances to show at the top of results pages than plain text only sites. An excellent way to present yourself to visitors on your site is a short video biography.

HASHTAGS

A keyword or phrase preceded by a hash symbol (#) is used within a post on social media to help people interested in a certain topic to find you when they search for a keyword or particular hashtag. Brand identity and awareness can be created by proper hashtag use. Hashtags are effective tools in the form of communication, for example on Instagram, which is an image-oriented platform.

Next to creating your own hashtag connected with your brand or company name, there are others that you can create to boost your chances of showing up in search results. For example, you can generate a hashtag for the specific purpose of being connected with your brand, in the form of some motivating short buzzword.

The best hashtags will always describe your present or future followers' lifestyle and interests, and never your attributes. Use situations or places where your followers would use your product to create a hashtag that will describe that situation.

BUILDING YOUR WEBSITE

The best move for digital personal branding is to create a website with your name, for example, *www.dariosipos.com*; investing in a domain of your name will appear professional. Additionally, it will be significant to SEO, and one day might lead to the ultimate result of having your own "Google Knowledge Panel".

That page will become one central online source for the single truth about you. Because you will decide how your brand feels and looks like on your personal website, your Google Knowledge Panel will become your central point containing all the information about your personal brand, including links to all your social networks.

Figure 21. Your personal website sits at the center of your online branding

First, you start with researching if your domain name is free. For that purpose, one of the best tools is *https://instantdomainsearch. com/* because it will check not only availability but numerous other possibilities and combinations of your desired name. When purchasing a domain, always use the .com domain because it will look global and be most SEO-friendly. Always register your full name or a minimum possible variation of your name.

After you registered your domain on your local domain selling service, you can usually purchase hosting from the same provider. The minimum size package will be sufficient for your needs. Once you buy hosting, ask the seller to install WordPress on the site and connect the domain with the hosting.

Now there are several ways to build your site. If your time is scarce and you have the extra budget, you can hire a web developer to create a site for you. Or, the cheapest and fastest method is to purchase a WordPress theme from the site as *www.themeforest.net*. Look for a WordPress theme using the keywords "personal portfolio" or "personal brand" or "CV". Choose the theme that most fits with your functionality needs and design wishes.

The only important parameters for the theme you choose are quality design, regular updates from the provider, and that it was sold more than just a few times, which indicates quality and good customer service. Also, the theme will have reviews so that you can see the opinion of other purchasers.

For a step-by-step guide on building your own website, visit *www. dariosipos.com/resources*.

As you already own the domain, you can create your email with *yourname@yourwebsite.com*, which will be more professional and rememberable.

Your site should have a section for your biography, personal interests, awards, societies or groups you are associated with, and your education and certifications.

There should be few calls to action in the form of "Contact me" or "Hire me to speak," depending on your career choice.

Every few weeks, ideally, or at least a few times per year, you should publish a small article (700-1200 words) from your expertise or interest area and then post it additionally through all your social media channels and other digital platforms.

There should be a separate section on your website for articles, but avoid using the headline "Blog" and use "Articles" instead. People prefer to read more articles and less of what they consider a personal blog.

Pages where you can find relevant articles and ideas for your site are aggregators of articles, such as *www.rightrelevance.com.*

Platform Medium on the site *www.medium.com* is the online publishing platform open to anyone, essentially a blogging platform. Medium is a place to share your stories and ideas with a broad and diverse audience with a straightforward, user-friendly publishing platform. It is an easy way to reach readers, and it can serve as your platform for publishing articles. It can also be a place to publish your articles before you have your website ready. Also, it is an excellent solution to publish articles even after you have your own website, to create more visibility and some more links to share on your social media. It is highly recommended that you open your account on the Medium platform and publish some content together with your short bio because it will add a layer to your digital presence.

ONLINE RESEARCH

How you look in the digital world is the same as how people who research you online will perceive you. The digital footprint that you leave behind you, after every action you take online, decides what content is displayed to you or who recommendation engines suggest you connect with on social media networks. To understand how the digital world sees you, the only method is to do online research of yourself. Then use the results to eliminate the irrelevant parts in your digital footprint and highlight the best of your brand online.

Therefore, it is crucial to use internet platforms often to do a thorough search to see what you can find about yourself online.

Google Alerts will be an effective way of getting notified whenever your name gets mentioned online. It will inform you via email that someone mentioned you in their posts, articles, or other media.

Before you do research, make sure you are using your preferred browser's incognito mode and log-out yourself from any platforms like Google and Gmail.

For search, it is possible to use either Google search, other crawlers' search functions, social network search window, or aggregators specialized in searching through several search engines at once. By using *www.dogpile.com*, you can get results for your search for the top three search engines without visiting them individually. Tools such as *www.social-mention.com* can be used to scan the landscape of social media for any mention of your name or subjects interesting to you.

Run a few variations of your search including: your name, email, phone number, user names from social media, and company/employer name. Collect all the information about you that you can find to either add to it, correct it, or remove it. Note down what you don't want to show on search and how social networks categorized you.

Notice the narrative that your research shows about you, and decide what information should be emphasized and what should be deleted.

Create one single bio for your personal digital brand and insert it in all social networks' bio sections. Cross-post the materials, articles, and posts which you are creating from one social network to another.

If there is content that you would like to delete but cannot, you can suppress it on search results by simply replacing it on search results with new activity. Instead of worrying about the old materials, simply create a lot of valuable new material that will show up on top of search results together with the narrative that shows your personal digital brand in a good light.

How to do that is by starting to write articles, creating your own website (domain with your name), interacting with the people online that you want to be associated with, and doing the same with companies. The more content you create about subjects you desire to be known for, the more it will appear on top of the search results.

Everyone will research you online sooner or later, usually before they even meet you. If not before, then after. When there is something negative about you online, you should confront it digitally in posts and blogs. Researching others before you meet them is a powerful tool to find out their interests and connections so that you can bring it up in the conversation. Everyone likes to speak about their interests, and the conversation will be more favorable for you.

SOCIAL MEDIA ALGORITHMS

Social media algorithms represent a complex way to do simple things. Complex in the sense that they are comprised of several hundred, if not thousands of, lines of code, all working to do something straightforward. Their function is to provide social media users with content that is personalized and relevant to them.

Facebook, Google, and virtually anyone running social media sites, know that users will only come back if they see what they like every time they log on. Algorithms are there to make that happen; they help ensure social media users aren't faced with content that is irrelevant to them.

Creating and publishing your content in a way that convinces social media algorithms that your content is relevant, will tell it to show and promote your content to the relevant audience. Sadly, this works both ways; if your content performs poorly in an algorithm relevance index, then it will be pushed to the back of the queue.

Despite their complexity, getting to grips with how social media algorithms work and developing ways to master them is not rocket science. In fact, most social media sites have clearly defined blueprints on how their algorithms handle 'signals' to dictate what gets shown and to whom it gets shown at any point.

From this and through experience, it is easy to map out a strategy that exploits these algorithms in your favor.

User Interaction Is a Huge Flag No Algorithm Will Miss

When your content gets people talking, you are promoting what social media sites want in the first place, which is interaction and user engagement. For that, you will be handsomely rewarded by their algorithms. It is important to note that algorithms track user interaction by measuring metrics like comments, likes, and shares.

Proven methods of pulling these metrics to your page are to create content that:

* Stimulates the interest of users
* Contains a call to action
* Speaks on a subject that users are passionate about
* Tags the people who matter

Social media hosts a deeply interconnected web of users. User A is connected to user B, and user B is connected to user C. Even though user C doesn't have a direct connection to user A, it's easy to see that a pathway for information spread – through user B – exists between user A and C.

The key takeaway here is that you do not necessarily need to be connected to everyone to reach everyone. Just one (or two, three) seeds is all it takes to make your social media forest flourish. So next time you create a post, make sure to tag influential users who relate with the content you are sharing. When you do that, you are shining a beacon for them (and everyone else linked to them) to see and interact with your content.

Timing Matters

There is such a thing as **peak hours** – the time when your audience base is most active on social media and **slow hours** – the period when they are mostly offline. Recognizing what time of the day these two periods fall under is the first step to making social media algorithms work for you.

That is because most social media algorithms are optimized to place a premium on time relevancy. They will want to show users more current information ahead of old posts. If most of your posts fall into the period when your users are offline, then they are more likely to land in the trash can of old posts. Avoid that by creating a social media timetable that takes peak hours into consideration.

The Bottom Line

Algorithms are there to pick out quality content from irrelevant content. Although one or two "black hat" methods to game the system might pop up once in a while, they are always short-lived. Worse still, they could get your content blacklisted. So, if you want to stay on top of algorithms, make sure to produce quality content consistently.

Consistency is critical for social media algorithms. For your audience to recognize your brand, you must be consistent. Being consistent in your social media brand allows you to grow audience engagement and reach, satisfying both users and algorithms.

Social shares are not the same as backlinks, but shares to the correct people may result in a backlink. Social shares increase traffic, visitors to your website increase brand awareness, and those two things result in the growth of trust and links. The connection between social signals and rankings is an indirect, yet essential part of the strategy.

The more you visit certain pages, the more search algorithms display similar content to you. It is important to be careful about your online presence and interactions with other content. Avoid leaving negatives reviews in your name, and set reviewing to private. Negative reviews, comments, or participation in unpolite conversations posted in your name will show up in search results.

SOCIAL MEDIA ALGORITHM PRINCIPLES

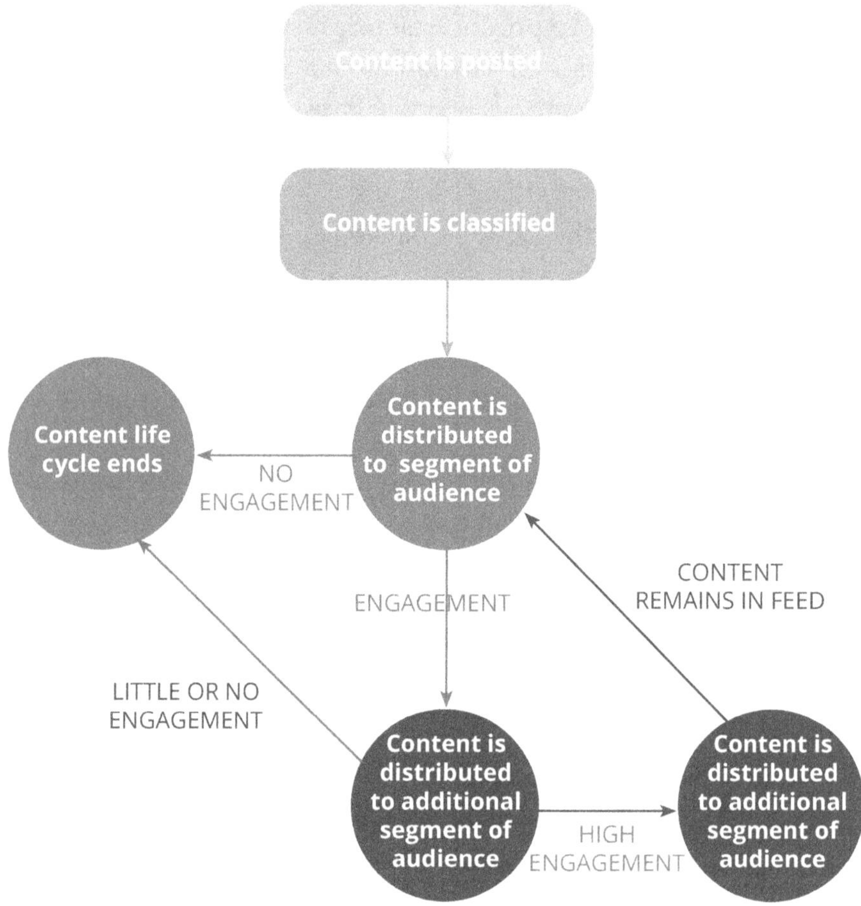

Figure 22. Social media algorithm principles

TOOLS FOR CONTENT CREATION

Some tools can help you create and publish content consistently and professionally:

* A content calendar
* Social media calendar software
* Graphic editor software
* WordPress templates
* Analytics software

We'll take a look at each of these tools in turn.

Content Calendar

A content calendar can be used to plan all content activity, including for social media. For example, publishing posts on blogs, forums, and all other available resources that you decide to use.

A content calendar can be a simple Excel file in a calendar-based format that will plan content as a rough sketch for a few weeks or months in advance.

Social Media Calendar Software

Consistency is crucial when publishing content on social media networks. Therefore, it is necessary to publish posts at regular, popular times for each network.

Social media calendar software will enable you to maximize and streamline your social media processes. In the purest form, the software will post on all of your social media profiles according to the schedule you put in place.

After you connect your social media profiles to the software, set up a posting schedule for each social media profile separately; you can fill software with posts for months in advance. In short, when you use such software, you can focus your social media efforts on quality instead of continually struggling to publish content at the correct time.

After publishing content, not only will it show you analytics on how well you did, but it will also store content in the archive, so, with a click of a button, you can re-publish it when needed.

Such software comes with a pretty low price while enabling the right amount of automatization. Some of the most commonly used social media calendars in the world are Buffer (*www.buffer.com*) and Hootsuite (*www.hootsuite.com*).

Graphics Editor Software

Graphic designers can create beautifully designed graphical material in different formats but are expensive, so they are not needed in this content creation process. That alone will save you a lot of money and time in your content creation process.

The material itself is not needed in high resolution, as it usually would be for printing, eliminating the need for high-quality purchased stock photos.

What is needed is a tool that can perform simple reformatting of posts for different social media networks. That can create many posts of similar nature with different free stock photos and text.

Such tools are: Canva (*www.canva.com*) with free and low-cost paid plans or the previously mentioned Buffer has an entirely free tool named Pablo (*pablo.buffer.com*), including 600,000 + stock photos for free.

When it comes to creating professional videos at a low cost, you can use tools such as Promo (*www.promo.com*), which offers customization of their massive database of professionally done videos, together with complex editing made simple in a straightforward interface.

All mentioned tools are designed so beginners can use them without any specialized knowledge.

WordPress Templates

Creating a website for your brand or creating a blog requires you to hire a web developer, an expensive and time-consuming endeavor. Because, for months, you will be communicating on design and development back and forth. Most of the websites today on the Internet, including many successful webshops, are designed in WordPress because it enables users to change and add content easily.

Almost all web developers buy premade templates from specialized sites at a low cost, ranging from $20–$59.

The largest depository of WordPress templates currently is ThemeForest (*www.themeforest.net*).

When you need to create a blog, brand page, or any type of page, first visit ThemeForest and compare the price with the quote you got from a web developer. No matter what type of site you wish to create, it's highly likely that it already exists, premade, easy to install, and at a low cost.

Analytics Software

To get data on what actually works as content for your personal brand, you need to use some of the Analytics Software options that will enable you to monitor interaction with your content, ideally to monitor all online interactions in one central console.

When you use any type of Social Media Calendar Software then it will already have included analytics by which you can monitor number of likes or shares on your social media posts. Interactions on social networks can be monitored inside the platforms as well.

For measuring website traffic to a WordPress website you can install a free plugin - Google Site Kit - which enables you to see all data on the website dashboard, or you can use Google Analytics externally. Google Analytics will tell you all about interactions with your website, including the demographics of visitors. The best performing organic content (not paid) can be used for paid-promotions, if you decide to invest more in your personal brand. For example, you might decide to promote your website (or services on your website) so you would pay Google Ads or Facebook Ads to bring more visits to your website; the best content to attract visitors through paid ads is obviously the content that already performs well organically.

CHAPTER 7

PERSONAL BRANDING ON SOCIAL MEDIA

All of us need to understand the importance of Branding. We are CEOs of our own companies: Me Inc. To be in business today, our most important job is to be head marketer for the brand called You.

Tom Peters

THE MOST IMPORTANT ROLES OF SOCIAL MEDIA

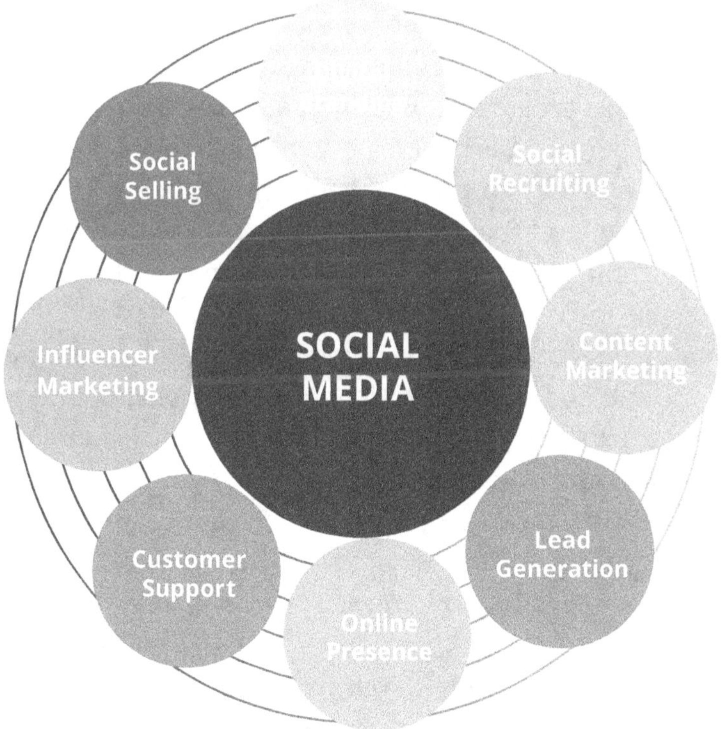

Figure 23. The most important roles of social media

LinkedIn

If you do not have any personal branding sites and are just starting your branding journey, start with LinkedIn. LinkedIn is the ultimate social media platform for sharing the right information with the right people.

A social media site for professionals with high popularity with the B2B audience is why the user base continues to grow. Members use the platform to expand their professional connections, showcase their companies, and search and apply for jobs. A LinkedIn feed is based on the people and topics you want to hear about. It makes it an excellent place for getting information on matters that affect your business and audience in the short and long term. With the LinkedIn advanced search settings, you can more precisely target the decision-makers.

LinkedIn is the world's largest social media network for professionals. All the people you need to reach to progress in your career or area of expertise are most likely already present on LinkedIn.

LinkedIn is the only social network that encourages business connections and discussions. First impressions on LinkedIn are created by the first impression of your profile and your first summary statement.

Because people create an impression about you online in the same way they do in person, it is necessary to fill in all the LinkedIn sections with clear statements and proof of your achievements. On the LinkedIn platform, the level to which you have filled your profile is ranked by grade "All-Star". That indicates that your profile has information that will enable it to rank higher than lower grades.

Your statements on LinkedIn should reflect who you are, what you do, what you can do for others, evidence of your claims, and who else confirms your expertise. LinkedIn is not only your resume. It is more of an essential communication tool.

The first results on LinkedIn that anyone who searches your name sees are your name, headline, photo, location, and industry. Your headshot photo needs to show you as approachable, professional, and yourself.

In the headline, space below your name, you shouldn't ever repeat your current position and employer. Because it is the most precious space that you have on your profile that people see first. The headline space below the name is currently limited to 120 characters, so you need to use it wisely.

Use headline space below your name to write a clear personal brand promise of your value. Headline space readers should be able to read what you can do for them. It should convey value and aspire to your future.

LinkedIn is considered a highly trusted site for search engines. It will most likely always come up in a high position in the search results. Search for yourself, check how your LinkedIn profile is displayed in the results, and then make necessary adjustments to show it in the best light possible.

In the summary section, you can tell your personal brand story by following storytelling guidelines and rules to make sure your story brings value to the readers (how to tell your brand story can be found in chapter 3).

Any successful story tells the reader how you will improve their lives or give them solutions to their questions. When writing the summary section, imagine you're having a conversation with your ideal reader. It is essential to show your personality in your story so that readers will connect and relate to you. Use testimonials and rich media (videos, photos, infographics) to clarify what you do.

When you write about your education or very old work positions, always write at least a sentence of what you learned or accomplished. When you add your education or work experience, always try to find and add the institution/company from the autosuggest typing box. Doing that will ensure the organization is represented on your profile with a link to its own verified profile. That adds credibility to your education and previous working positions. It backs up your claims and provides clarity and transparency to visitors of your profile.

Most educational institutions and companies have their own LinkedIn presence. In that way, people will be able to see they are real, and your network will expand by association. You can always connect with other people who went to the same educational institution or worked at the same company by checking the section on the organization's profile and listing "all employees" or "all alumni".

In the contact section, you can add your website links or links to other sites that you are affiliated with. On LinkedIn, you can customize your URL to match your name and not contain any numbers in it, which is how it is displayed at the beginning. That will be easier to display on your other social media profiles and more memorable.

In other sections, you can add the projects on which you worked and add members of the team, which then confirms your claims.

The best feature of LinkedIn is the ability to collect or give recommendations to others. Ask your colleagues or management for the recommendations without hesitation because you can choose which you wish to display on your profile. By offering recommendations to others, you will also get into a position to receive them.

Another option of LinkedIn is to gather skill endorsements from your network; here, they don't have to write a recommendation which requires more effort so it may increase your chances of receiving lots of endorsements. Endorsements are less valuable than recommendations because you choose from a list of skills. Then members of your current network are asked to endorse them. Currently, on LinkedIn it is even possible to pass exams for areas that you claim you have expertise. For example, if you pass the exam directly on LinkedIn for "Google Analytics," the certificate will show itself on your profile. It will be an indicator to everyone that you really do have knowledge of the area you claimed. The exams are not so easy to pass, and it is possible to try passing them only two times. Always limit skills to a modest number and keep the top skills necessary for your career or future on the top. You can freely re-sort the order of your top endorsed skills.

LinkedIn Social Selling Index Score

LinkedIn has a tool, the Social Selling Index (SSI), to measure the activity and ranking of LinkedIn member's activity. Based on much research by LinkedIn, the higher SSI will bring you more opportunities in business.

You can measure your SSI by going to URL: *https://www.linkedin.com/sales/ssi* while being logged into your LinkedIn account.

In simple terms, the SSI score shows your social selling engagement.

LinkedIn calculates SSI score based on establishing your professional brand, finding the right people, engaging with insights, and building relationships. It means that you should improve your SSI score by spending 10 minutes a day working on the mentioned pillars.

Just because you are online, nothing will change for you. It is still all about knowing the right people through networking. The purpose of SSI is to indicate to you which areas you need to improve so members of your network will view you as an expert.

TWITTER

Twitter is a social network that works as a microblogging platform where users are limited to 280 characters per post, called a tweet. The primary idea of Twitter is to enable people to share their thoughts with a big audience but centered around real-time conversation. Twitter is much less focused on social friendships but more on allowing people to follow important topics, people, and discussions that are relevant to them. People on Twitter are less connected than those on Facebook, for example. For instant news, Twitter is the best network to use. Twitter has only a short bio section, so you will be ready to use it in no time.

Twitter is the easiest platform to become an expert by creating content about your expertise. Where you can provide value to your followers and build your community of followers.

Find fresh, authoritative, and relevant content to share from specialized news and article generator sites. One such site that works exceptionally well is Right Relevance (*www.rightrelevance.com*), which offers free account registration.

Twitter is the primary channel for journalists and media and is very popular in the USA, UK, and gradually getting more popular in other countries too.

One of the best features of Twitter is how easy it is to find people to follow. You can also find local Twitter users and, by engaging with them, create your first network.

Twitter offers "people similar to you" and "who to follow" suggestions based on a few combined parameters about your activity so that you can connect with similar-minded people.

When you start creating useful content and following people, you will also get followers.

Don't forget to join the conversation by retweeting, replying, or saving favorite comments.

FACEBOOK

Facebook has many features that are perfect for personal branding, primarily because they are designed to share different types of content that will help you to tell your story in an engaging way.

On Facebook you can be social while also sharing your personal brand information and expertise.

Facebook will shape your reputation in the same way it would be formed in an offline community, by the way you behave, people you associate with, information that you share, and information that others share about you.

Facebook is one of the best platforms to reach a larger audience and the largest social media site considering the number of members. Currently, Facebook dominates the digital marketing space.

Use analytics for targeting a specific audience and proper timing of the posts. Figure out the best schedules for your posts through trial and error. At: *www.dariosipos.com/resources* you can find some best practice tips on timing.

Using lots of images is a great tactic. The chances of a user clicking on your post increases drastically when you use high-quality images. Here we don't mean a "high-quality resolution," but an image showing fun or useful content.

Motivate your audience to participate by keeping your posts fun and entertaining. When a post is compelling, it is more likely to be shared.

Instead of focusing on only getting likes, create pools, or multiple-choice questions. Create questions in such a way that the audience will be motivated to add their vote.

Focusing solely on your personal brand will not create a friendly, relatable relationship with the audience. Post some content about other brands that share similar values.

Facebook also allows you to create a brand page in addition to your personal page. It's best to use both of these options; keep your personal page for creating meaningful connections and your brand page to represent you in a more serious light. On a brand page you can create and post materials only about your expertise, similar to your LinkedIn page.

A short checklist of things every Facebook brand page should have is:
* Customized URL
* Welcome message to direct first-time visitors to your page
* List of all your other social media profiles
* Complete informative "About" section with your overall business information, awards, achievements, and your brand story

Niche Facebook Groups are an excellent spot for any person to market their services and bring awareness to their brand. Although niche groups already contain an audience that is very interested in certain products, avoid being aggressive with promotion. A better method is to take part in discussions and offer solutions only when they are visibly needed.

Managing the brand page on Facebook is a daily task that needs to be done systematically, because trends are continually changing and Facebook quite often changes how users can see your messages.

INSTAGRAM

Instagram has become a crucial marketing and sales opportunity for any type of business, especially in regards to the younger generation. It is often described as a holy grail for small business due to its ability to drive sales on a low budget while being scalable. That dynamic audience makes it perfect for personal branding purposes.

Instagram is primarily an image sharing site, which means that you need to focus on your visuals. Offer visually likable content that is interesting.

Use Instagram Stories because they are entertaining, habit creating, and you can easily personalize it to your personal brand by simply showing what you are doing behind the scenes daily.

Instagram is very well accepted among younger generations. Therefore, if you are an executive, you can significantly support employee participation by using Instagram.

IGTV (Instagram TV) gives you a longer format so you can present for longer.

Posting often is essential. It is crucial to stay active and give it more attention than some other channels may require.

Communicate with people, engage with them. People will like your content because you like their content.

Products need to be shown through engaging content, which does not focus only on you. Eye-Catching images are essential: Instagram is fundamentally a platform where customers search for purchase inspiration.

Use hashtags to target subjects your ideal audience might be interested in. Create your own hashtags and engage with people to encourage its use.

Find the perfect timing by using some free online software to see which tags and filters have the best correlation to comments on posts.

To reach a specific audience among such a great number of people using the platform, use hashtags, mentions, and stories.

The reason that Instagram is such an excellent tool for your personal brand is that it uses photos as a primary way of communication. Photos are the best thing in marketing because they:

* Make you more relatable
* Are engaging
* Make more emotional connection than just text

User-generated content is an excellent method to build a community around your brand. So when your personal brand grows do your best to convince followers to submit their own photos, which you can then feature on your feed or Instagram Story.

One of the major ways to be successful on Instagram is to create your own original content and then consistently share it with your followers.

On Instagram, content is everything, so make your personal brand stand out using the following methods:

* Posting consistently and frequently to grab viewers' attention
* Visually attractive posts will attract more attention

* Create a theme for your brand page, through color, pattern, and filters
* Speak with a tone of communication that matches your audience
* Invest plenty of effort in writing captions and researching hashtags

Instagram Stories are images and videos that users can upload, which disappear after some time if not saved permanently to a "highlight". Using as many features as possible on Instagram Stories will make content more engaging.

When managing stories, the best results will have:
* A length of fifteen seconds
* Questions and polling features to drive engagement
* Stickers and emojis to create more exciting content
* A consistent timeline of daily posts
* A set of important stories saved to highlights so they are permanently visible

Influencer marketing, a modern-day version of word-of-mouth marketing, is one of the most essential ways of making your brand visible on Instagram.

When you create a strong visual brand on Instagram, build a community around it, and start using all social selling options available, then your personal brand will get strong engagement, and a more significant community.

YouTube

As one of the first social media channels that came into existence, YouTube is not only a place to watch videos but it is also the second-largest search engine in the world.

YouTube is an effective channel to build brand awareness and connect your target customers to your brand. If you can create interesting content, then you have more chances to create engagement. The benefit of YouTube over traditional media, such as TV, is that you can create good-enough content even with your phone camera. The key takeaways to manage the channel successfully are:

* When you create videos, they should always be one of these three types: Entertaining, Educational, or Inspiring.
* Start by creating videos of three to four minutes, any longer and the audience will lose interest.
* Create videos in advance, so you will always stick to your video publishing calendar. Consistently demonstrate your value and strive to have a smart and straightforward video that makes a great story but based on a simple concept.
* When you have a video of longer duration, make short thirty-second trailers out of it and post them on other platforms. In this way, you can repurpose the video on other social media channels and still drive viewers to see it on YouTube.
* Investing in equipment is a good idea, especially when it comes to sound, lighting, and editing software. A basic lightning set will dramatically increase the quality of your recorded video material.

Growing a large, engaged audience takes time and consistent effort, so get ready for it by creating and writing down your long-term strategy without expecting sudden success. Decide on why you are creating videos. Is it to increase brand awareness, or to increase sales, or to show customers how products work? Decide on a theme and key messages.

The section below the video is a precious place to add your links or a coupon code for sales. Including descriptions, other channels, or information on how to contact you is crucial.

YouTube has its own SEO ranking algorithm, which is similar to Google. Using keywords, titles, hashtags, and writing a good description will help generate more traffic.

Videos represent an extraordinary opportunity for success on social media. Years ago, you would require a team of professionals and a huge budget to create a single video, but today you can create it by using a phone camera combined with some user-friendly editing software. In that way, you can create great looking and meaningful videos in-house for a fraction of the cost and compete successfully with large brands.

PINTEREST

Pinterest is a powerful virtual corkboard and the ultimate platform for searching for inspiration and planning projects. Most users know it as a visual discovery tool and a catalog of ideas. Any content you make should not be disruptive to the user's experience. People that visit Pinterest are looking for inspiration and ideas. You can inspire them by creating your virtual corkboard where you will post about subjects on which you are an expert.

The reason to choose Pinterest for personal branding is that Pins you create can rank rather high on Google for your name's searches. It will not suppress your main results like your personal webpage, social media platforms, or news mentions. Still, it will provide the searcher with additional context about your expertise.

Because Pinterest is different than other social networks, it is highly recommended that you read the user manual help section of Pinterest because it explains simply how to operate the platform to maximum effect.

Pinterest is more than just a social network. It contains its own powerful search engine. Map out the keywords that are important for you. When you post a picture by creating a pin, you will need to write text to accompany it, including mapped keywords and hashtags.

Focus on creating or sharing excellent content because Pinterest is about smooth gliding through relevant content. Posts need to be optimized for mobile because 82% of users are on the mobile app.

You will have the best results when you create themed boards that are a mixture of inspirational Pins with practical ones. In that way, you will create an organic targeted audience that will save specific Pins.

When you read anything interesting on the web with good visual content like photos, infographics, or videos, you can pin it to your board.

Try to Pin every day or every other day; as much as possible, make Pins lead to your site because pinning consistently produces the most difference. You will increase your personal brand awareness by pinning stunning images and also attract new followers by using Pins to serve new ideas with useful information.

Quora

One of the largest social networks where people ask and answer questions about hundreds of topics and categories. When Google doesn't give you detailed enough customized answers, post it on Quora under a relevant category to get a response. Then you can even send an answer request to topic experts. Quora is a platform where you can connect with people who contribute quality answers, and in that way, build a community around your topic that touches your personal brand.

Quora is best used when you want to convince a large crowd of people that you are a high-level expert without promotional messaging. Because the platform covers so many questions across vast topics, it is easy to find questions where you will be able to answer based on your expertise. In your answers it's easy to link off-platform material like links to sites. That is a great method to driving traffic to your personal website.

Quora is easy to start, it can be connected to Twitter so that whenever you post an answer on Quora, it gets tweeted automatically.

After you fill your profile with as much information as possible, you need to search for questions that need to be answered. You are allowed to post content that promotes some services but only if it is relevant to the questions asked.

To get to the top of search results on Quora, your answers should be upvoted by other users. Upvoted answers are considered by Quora algorithms as useful and then promoted on the platform.

Suppose your answer was upvoted by large number of users. In that case, it might even get into Quora Digest, a newsletter with the highest trending answers.

When answering questions, avoid too much professional language, explain complex answers in clear and understandable sentences.

Quora will demonstrate your expertise and elevate your digital personal brand.

SlideShare

SlideShare is an excellent content marketing platform, which most people have never used or heard about. It is a high-ranking site with above sixty million visitors per month and eighty million users.

On SlideShare, you can upload presentations about your expertise. They will show up high on search results when someone researches your name.

Because the site is popular among professionals but not widely used by other audience, the result is a highly visited site with low competition.

Google considers SlideShare to be a high authority website, which means it will rank high on the search results. That means SlideShare can create a significant positive difference in your online ranking.

Presentations that are uploaded need to be excellent to attract visitors. Therefore, you need to work on your content.

When you upload your presentation to SlideShare, you need to start promoting it on all your other platforms.

SlideShare doesn't allow links in the presentation description, so you have to insert links in your presentation if you wish readers to visit your personal websites or social media profiles.

Because people rarely click on links, you need to create a good call to action with a reason why readers would click on it, clarifying the benefits of them doing so.

When you have a website, you can embed your presentation on it easily, which serves to build backlinks from your website to SlideShare and vice versa. Whenever you write articles, especially on LinkedIn, you can easily embed your presentation.

The most useful integration is between SlideShare and Twitter because it adds tweet buttons on your presentations. In that way, people who tweet your presentation will mention you. Other social network integrations simply help to share your presentations more easily.

CHAPTER 8

CREATING CONTENT AND NETWORKING

You deserve a circle of inclusion and influence, but it's up to you to create it.

Richie Norton

CREATING AND DEPLOYING CONTENT

Before creating content, it is important to answer these questions, because the answers are the core of your personal brand online:

* What are you known for?
* What are the values you stand for?
* What do you want to be known for?
* What makes you different?
* What are your areas of expertise?
* What kind of problems do you solve?
* How do you demonstrate your contribution?
* How have you been successful in the past?
* What are your professional achievements?
* Who are your role models?
* Who should know about you?

By answering these questions, you will determine your core value and the direction of your personal brand communications.

DEPLOYING CONTENT

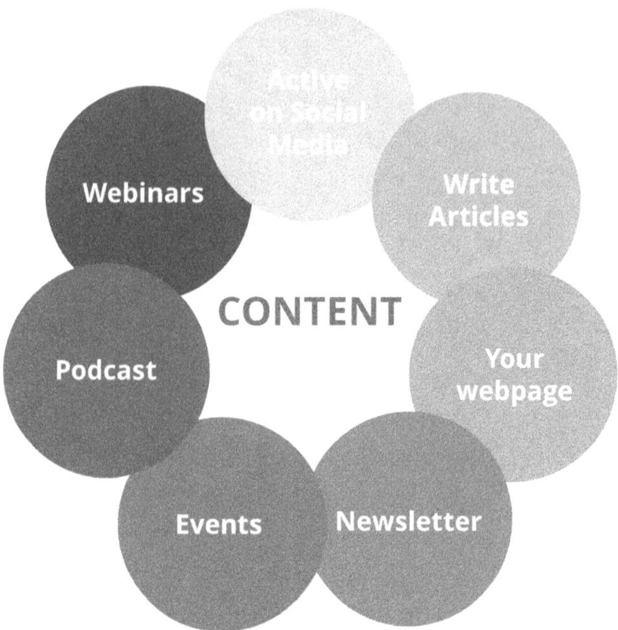

Figure 24. Deploying content

Just after you have created your website and social media profiles, you can start writing articles and posts.

When writing articles, be creative within a topic and try to connect with your reader. Always write in the first person, and engage readers by asking them their opinion. Always insert what you are passionate about into articles, no matter what your actual occupation is. The ideal length of articles is 700–1200 words. Just because you post something online, it doesn't mean it will get comments, so try to engage readers by asking them to leave a comment or leave a question in the article and posts. Answer any comments promptly.

Answering comments and engaging with your audience is the stepping stone to building your community.

When you start publishing you need to do it consistently and regularly. You should create and post articles every few weeks, and you should publish social media posts a few times per week. In a post you can share relevant information from your area of expertise. When writing, the content needs to be around the topic for which you are an expert.

The first article on your website should be an introduction to what you are writing about and why. Make it so that the introduction article always stays pinned at the top, so first-time visitors can easily find and read it first.

Your writing needs to incorporate your personality and passions.

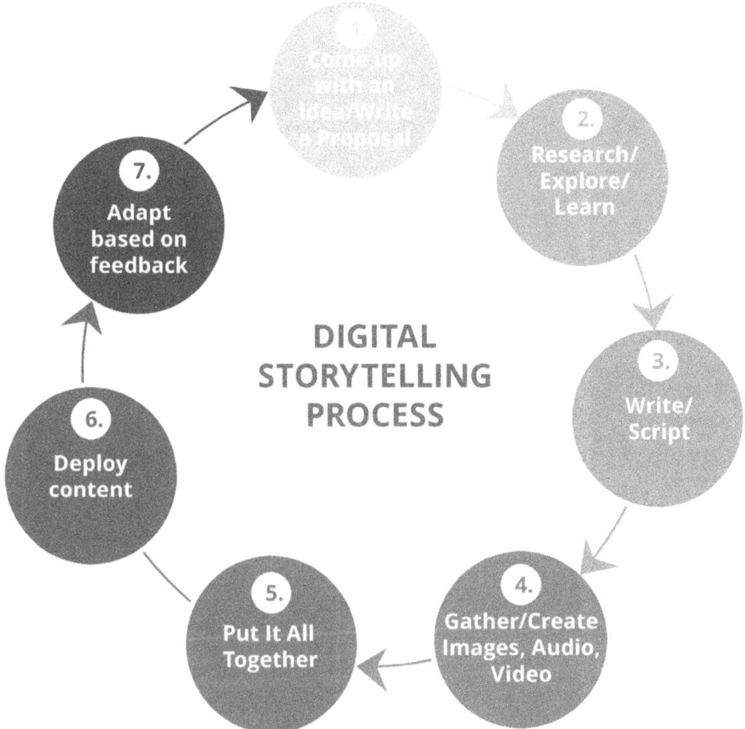

Figure 25. Digital storytelling process

Steps in creating and deploying content:

1. After you have come up with an idea, write a proposal outlining what the content will be about and your aims.
2. Research the topic of your content.
3. Write your article or script your video/audio.
4. Find and gather all the supporting images, audio and video for the content piece.
5. Finalise the content.

6. Post article on your website, on Medium.com, or as a LinkedIn article. Reshare that article on your social media. Ask the readers to comment.
7. Based on feedback adapt and repeat steps.

Figure out what you want to communicate and then do it consistently by using all possible digital communication tools.

Here are some ideas on how and where you can deliver your message:

* Create your own website
* Write articles
* Start a podcast or contribute to another
* Interview others
* Publish PR releases
* Create infographics
* Start a social media group
* Join a professional association
* Do webinars/online conferences
* Speak at conferences
* Run workshops
* Offer teaching
* Create program reviews
* Answer questions on Quora

Podcasting

Podcasting is perfect for personal branding because of how it is transferred to audiences easier than text or video. Podcasts can be listened to while doing other tasks and, thanks to smartphones, they can be consumed anywhere.

Podcasting fits perfectly into personal branding because of the intimate atmosphere and bond it creates with the listener; it can feel like the speaker and listener personally know each other. For personal branding the current most well working trend is podcasting.

Video

Video does a great job grabbing the attention of users on social media because it is more engaging than text.

Articles

Articles are great for showcasing your knowledge and expertise. They are essential for establishing yourself as a thought leader.

Infographics

Infographics are a visual representation of information, data, or knowledge, which can be used to share data and statistics, or visualize content. They are very effective for personal branding because they provide educational content while being highly sharable.

NETWORKING ON THE INTERNET

Just because we are talking about online personal branding doesn't mean everything we know about offline personal branding doesn't apply; it is still all about knowing the right people through networking. After you've updated your digital presence, it is time to network, nurture relationships, and increase your visibility to get people to notice you.

Networking is how to achieve star status in digital personal branding. In the digital world your network depends on your effort, and the more time you invest in it, the more valuable it will be. Social media networking will accelerate any career.

Any conversation online is guided by social media algorithms because they decide who sees your message, if your message ends up in spam, or which news you see in your social media feed. Algorithms are a great thing because they recommend connections based on similar interests, enabling more efficient networking.

In digital networking, the best position to be in is when someone you wish to connect with has already seen you online. You can simply comment on their posts, like their content, or participate in the same online conversations.

When you reach out to people on LinkedIn, they will most likely respond – if they don't, they are probably just buried under other messages.

In order for your connection requests to be accepted quickly you must have a fully up-to-date profile, complete with contact information because that will add to your credibility.

In creating posts quality is what matters, not quantity. Usually, more frequent posts result in lower quality.

As a professional you should only post when you want to share content that you created, respond about the content, when you want to share an opinion, communicate some question, or congratulate someone. All content that you publish should add some value.

In the digital world – and in the real world – you should communicate equally well with anyone, no matter if they are professionally important to you or just a student who is starting their career.

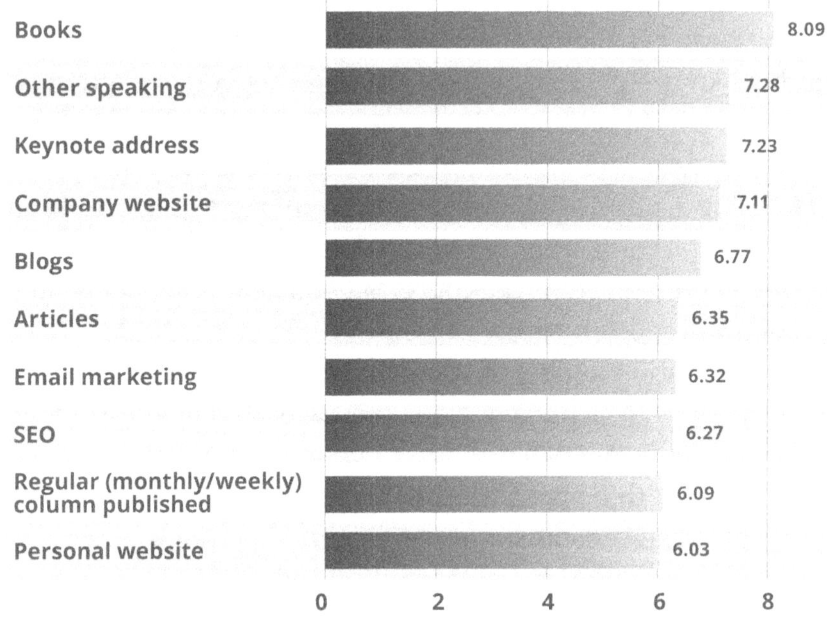

Figure 26. Branding tools by share of total impact for creating leads about your expertise (Hinge Research Institute, USA, 2021)

According to research done by Hinge Research Institute, the best five tools for personal branding that will return the most networking and new opportunities once when you create them are:

1. Books
2. Online videos

3. Blog/website posts
4. News articles
5. Keynote addresses

Using these content marketing methods, you will expand your visibility and expertise.

Note that your personal website, in Figure 26, is on the bottom of the list for creating new opportunities. At the same time for successful digital personal branding, your personal website is the first thing that should be created. Your personal website will contain the complete story about you, and be the single source of truth that you then transfer to all other means of communication with the public.

We can summarize digital personal branding efforts universally in the Personal Branding Matrix.

PERSONAL BRAND PRESENCE	REPUTATION MANAGEMENT	WHAT STRATEGY YOU USE?	THOUGHT LEADERSHIP
How do you create your brand online ?	How are you displayed online?	What strategy you use?	How do you create credibility online ?
Personal Brand Text with Keywords + Branded Biography	Authority website + URL formula: [first name] + [last name] .com + Personal URL on Social Media	Keywords Identification	PR & Media Outreach + Bloggers + Influencers + Magazines
Positioning of Personal Brand + Messaging + Audience	LinkedIn + Completed Profile + Networking	Writting Articles	Recognition and Awards
Brand Identity + Headshots + Other Images	Search Engines + Google Alerts + Update information	Articles and eBooks	Speaking + Workshops + Conferences + Webinars
Style of Communication + Substance + Style of Communication + Reputation	Social Media + Facebook + Twitter + Pinterest + Instagram + Other Social Media	Podcasting + Social Media Content + Infographics + Videos	Good Causes + Teaching + Helping Others

Figure 27. Personal Branding Matrix

SIX WARNING SIGNS THAT YOU ARE CREATING IRRELEVANT CONTENT

The phrase "content is king" was coined shortly after search engines came into existence. At that time, all that content publishers needed to do to be successful was to flood the Internet with as much content as they could create. Pushing out as much content as possible – like casting many nets at sea – was the sure-fire way to pull in the haul (read: internet traffic). Or so they thought.

As it turns out, pushing out content in droves was not the secret to driving engagement. For that, you will need a healthy dose of informative, educational, and, more importantly, relevant content. To help guide your steps and help keep you within the confines of relevance, here are six warning signs that pop up when you are producing irrelevant content.

Your Content Is Not Picking Up Organic Steam

How much organic engagement do your publications attract on their own? If the number is towards the lower limit of the average traffic statistic for your niche, then you are most likely producing content that is inapplicable to your audience. In other words, it is irrelevant.

You must understand just what your audience wants. When you publish content that falls outside the scope of audience interest, it is less likely to convert into clicks regardless of how superb your content is. It makes no sense, for instance, to throw scientific articles at an audience that is begging for a daily dose of celebrity gossip.

It Fails Grossly at Answering Any Specific Questions

The Internet, and more especially search engines, are filled with users searching for answers to a myriad of questions. It is no surprise that the vast bulk of Google search queries revolve around "how-tos", "where-tos", and "what-tos". When you produce content with an intent to strike the bells of relevancy, it should ideally provide answers to the questions members of your target audience are most likely to pose.

You Have Visitors All Right, But None of Them Stay for Long Enough
The amount of time visitors spend on your content, measurable with key performance indicators (KPIs) like bounce rates and time-on-page, paints a vivid picture of how relevant your content is to the viewing audience. If they spend very little time, indicated by a high bounce rate, then it means you have failed to grab their attention. If your content is not getting their attention, then it is, by all means, irrelevant to them.

Your Search Engine Ranking Is Tumbling
Search engine algorithms pay keen attention to vital signals that point them to what people like to see. If people shy away from your content (indicating that it is irrelevant to them), search engine algorithms take note. And the penalty for that is that your publications get relegated to the end of the list, far off from the top of the search rankings.

So, next time you search for keywords you have blended into your content and your page fails to turn up in search engine listings reassess yourself, it could be that the material was irrelevant in the first place.

Your Keywords Don't Reflect Your Audiences' Habits
In drumming up a viable content strategy, it is easy to fall down the rabbit hole of creating keywords that sound good to you as opposed to those that mirror your audience's search patterns. For instance, when targeting a person who wants to be a digital marketing expert, it seems that "digital marketing expert" would be a valid keyword, when in reality those people were mostly searching for things like "how to set up social media". Publishers who fail to incorporate key-word research as part of their content creation strategy usually make this mistake. Often, the result is irrelevant content.

It's Simply Not Unique
If your content appears to be a toned-down mash-up of what is available elsewhere on the Internet, then you are merely providing your audience with what they are already tired of seeing. Internet users want something unique, a different perspective on that subject of debate, advice that goes beyond cookie-cutter, or news that is broken

first by you. When you are able to provide them with a relatable spectrum of any of these information sets, then you are well set up to sail through their subconscious relevance filter.

The common theme that can be inferred from these signs (and their underlying causes) is that content drummed up without putting the audience in perspective will not appeal to its target audience. If your goal is to get people hooked, you need to know what they want and how they want it presented.

CHAPTER 9

ADVANCED DIGITAL PERSONAL BRANDING

Google only loves you when everyone else loves you first.
Wendy Piersall

ADVANCED TYPES OF SOCIAL MEDIA

In previous chapters, we mentioned all the steps necessary to build an excellent online presence for your personal digital brand using core media types.

There are more advanced methods and tactics that we will study in this chapter so you can really uplift your personal brand in search results.

When people hear "social media," they usually have in mind the most prominent social networks (Twitter, Facebook, LinkedIn) together with media sharing sites (Instagram, YouTube). There is much more to social media than only the top few that people use to connect online.

We can group social media based on their and users' purposes:

* **Social Networks** – Connecting with people, and catching up on news (Facebook, LinkedIn, Twitter)
* **Media Sharing Networks** – Share photos, videos, other rich media (Instagram, Snapchat, YouTube)
* **Bookmarking and Content Curation Networks** – Discover, save, and share content (Pinterest, Flipboard)
* **Discussion Forums** – Share ideas and news (Quora, Reddit, Digg)
* **Interest-based Networks** – Share interests and hobbies (Goodreads, Last.fm)

* **Publishing and Blogging Networks** – Publish content online (Medium, WordPress, Tumblr)
* **Social Shopping Networks** – Shop Online (Etsy, Fancy)
* **Anonymous Social Networks** – Communicate Anonymously (Ask.fm, Whisper)
* **Sharing Economy Networks** – Trade goods and services (Uber, Airbnb)
* **Consumer Review Networks** – Review and locate businesses (TripAdvisor, Trustpilot)

When you sort social media into categories and pay attention when new platforms arrive on the market, you will understand current trends and how people's attention shifts. From current trends and lists of social media types, you can get new ideas and channels for engaging with your potential audience. Depending on what you do and with whom you want to communicate, you can always find the idea to communicate even using social media type, that isn't the first logical choice. For example, do not limit yourself to a social media platform that is the obvious choice, but explore other social media types that are not commonly used in your niche. Using channels that others in your field are not using will make your personal brand more unique, therefore, more visible.

So next to the core social media types mentioned in previous chapters that are the base for your personal brand, you should always focus on finding any possible new platform, including the ones mentioned above, but also new social media apps as they appear on the market. This way you will really dominate the search results.

Wikipedia

The pinnacle of digital personal branding is having your own Wikipedia page because it will help you maintain your online reputation, get exposure, and add credibility to anything you are doing. Even though anyone can open a Wikipedia page, it is very hard to keep it running if you did not do anything significant backed up by years of references, it will get deleted very quickly. Wikipedia is managed by its members and administrators, who will delete a page not deemed worthy for the site.

Sources to support your content on Wikipedia that qualify include:
* Books
* Newspapers
* Magazines
* Journals

Sources that do not qualify:
* Social Media
* Press releases
* Professional/personal blogs

So, in order to be able to create a Wikipedia page, you have to have a lot of mentions in other formats such as news appearances, books, and similar types of materials that will prove you deserve to have a Wikipedia page. After years of dedicated work on your personal digital brand, you can certainly collect enough success and references that will enable you to have a Wikipedia page built.

Until then, you can open your profiles on sites that are very similar to Wikipedia but have less strict rules, for example:
* Everipedia.com profile
* Wikialpha.com profile
* Everybodywiki.com

Next to that, it is highly recommended to open your personal profile on Crunchbase.com, which is very intuitive and easy to do. Crunchbase is a place designed to discover innovative companies and the people involved with them, so quite a popular place for discovering accurate information on often secretive companies.

Be on the lookout for different online places and apps you can join that will help you leave a digital trail, the way you want it to appear. Do not forget to document online any good society or charity role that you do in your personal life outside of the online world. Find such opportunities to help people, then help them for real, and use social media to draw awareness to the issues so others might help too.

SEARCH ENGINE PRESENCE AND RESULTS

Google Knowledge Panel is the block that appears on the right side of the screen in the search results. It is created when the search engine connects all types of data that Google finds for a search term on the web. Google Knowledge Panel is a result of what is known as Google Knowledge Graph, which displays images, text, and social media links. If you work on your digital branding in a systematic way, and you published enough online material, and if you have a website, publications, and similar content, you will eventually get a personal panel. Then you can influence what Google displays in the panel.

If you wish to be found for search terms like your name, then the Google Knowledge Panel is a great option. Once Google displays it that means you are dominating search results on the right side of the search.

Knowledge Panel will make your personal brand stand out in the search results and will result in a lot of visibility.

There is no process by which you could request a personal panel. Instead, Google decides if you deserve a Knowledge Panel based on if your brand has enough authority online. Well-known people have a lot of online material, including different profile pages such as Wikipedia.

After some persistent work, Google will offer you the option to claim your Knowledge Panel. The information that it will show will arrive from different places such as Wikipedia, LinkedIn, Facebook, Crunchbase, and others. Any information that Google deems truthful and accurate is stored in Google Knowledge Graph.

It's best to have a Knowledge Panel that will fill with information in small increments, because that will make it stable. If you have a Wikipedia page, then the first sentence on Google Knowledge Panel will be your first Wikipedia sentence, but if you do not have a stable Wikipedia page and it gets deleted, then that will affect your Knowledge Panel. Deletion of your Wikipedia page will indicate to Google that you do not deserve a Knowledge Panel. In summary, Google needs to see confirmation of information about you in multiple locations.

Google Alerts is an effective way of getting notified whenever your brand gets mentioned online. It will inform you via email that someone mentioned you in their posts, articles, or other media. In that way, you know that your efforts are bringing results.

When you build your own webpage, you need to install WordPress plugins such as Yoast or Squirrly that will create schema of a page. Schema markup is a type of data that is added to your website to give search engines a summary and overview of the page. That will then feed into Google Knowledge Graph and participate in making your Knowledge Panel.

Having a Google Knowledge Panel indicates that Google understands what you do and who you are. That will give you influence in the world.

ORGANIC AND PAID CONTENT PROMOTION

After you've done all that you can organically with your social media and other online efforts, you might decide that you need additional awareness by paying for search engine advertising or social media advertising.

It's essential to understand the differences between organic and paid promotions and how they influence each other.

Organic traffic is the term used to describe visits to a website coming from a search engine's organic results and not from paid ads.

After users enter a query in a search engine (such as Google or Bing), they are presented with a set of results that include both the pages ranking on the top positions organically and a set of ads (usually denoted with the word "Ad") to differentiate them from the organic results.

After a user clicks on organic search results leading them to a website, then that action is recorded in an analytic tool as organic search traffic.

The most crucial difference in comparing paid to organic traffic is that the former is paid, and the latter is free.

There are two ways to get traffic from search engines. Your website can be ranked high in the search results, or you could pay for an ads service (such as Google Ads) to place your ads on top of the organic results with advertising.

With organic traffic, you can get visits to your website as long as you rank high enough for users to see your site on search engine results pages. On the other hand, with paid traffic, visits will drop as soon as you stop paying for ads. Therefore, by paying for ads, you are just temporarily renting attention. Whereas with organic efforts, you create permanent results in search engine rankings.

Additionally, the better the organic rank your website has, the less you will have to pay for ads to promote it.

By creating great content, you will acquire high-quality off-site signals, which will be interpreted by search engines as brand and industry authority, and eventually will lead to visibility. If you do not have a broad audience, then even superior content has to be pushed to be discovered. Content promotion is crucial for bringing your content to new online audiences and eventually earn you the traffic and conversions, which is your ultimate SEO goal.

Content that you create should position you as a thought leader, but not as a hero, in the eyes of your potential customers and audience. Increased off-site signals increase domain authority and search visibility. To earn these signals, it is necessary to create and promote content that is valuable enough to be shared.

There are a variety of channels where you can do content promotion, and new ones appear often. Channels for content promotion can be email, webinars, social media networks, blogs, and others. Opportunities to promote content are endless.

Naturally, you should publish your content on Facebook, but also you should spend significant time finding out where your current and potential customers spend time online additionally.

Content promotion needs to be used in order to reach a new audience and connect with them: If you do not reach new audiences, you cannot grow your audience. For example, if you manage your Instagram account by merely publishing content to existing followers without reaching a new audience, then your follower count will stay low forever.

Content promotion brings website traffic, improves engagement, and convinces potential customers to do business with you. It will help to communicate the value you provide and to nurture relationships, creating word-of-mouth promotions in turn.

Each channel has its own advertising system. To learn how each channel functions, the best method is to read the help section of each platform or visit one of many available free classes online. All the platforms contain help sections that will guide you on how to successfully use them, especially in regards to paid promotions.

It is crucial that you get your education from multiple sources but always strive to get it directly from the platform owner as a first step. No person will be able to tell you better which data entry fields needs to be filled in the Facebook ads than Facebook itself.

Let's summarize all five types of media where you can promote your brand:

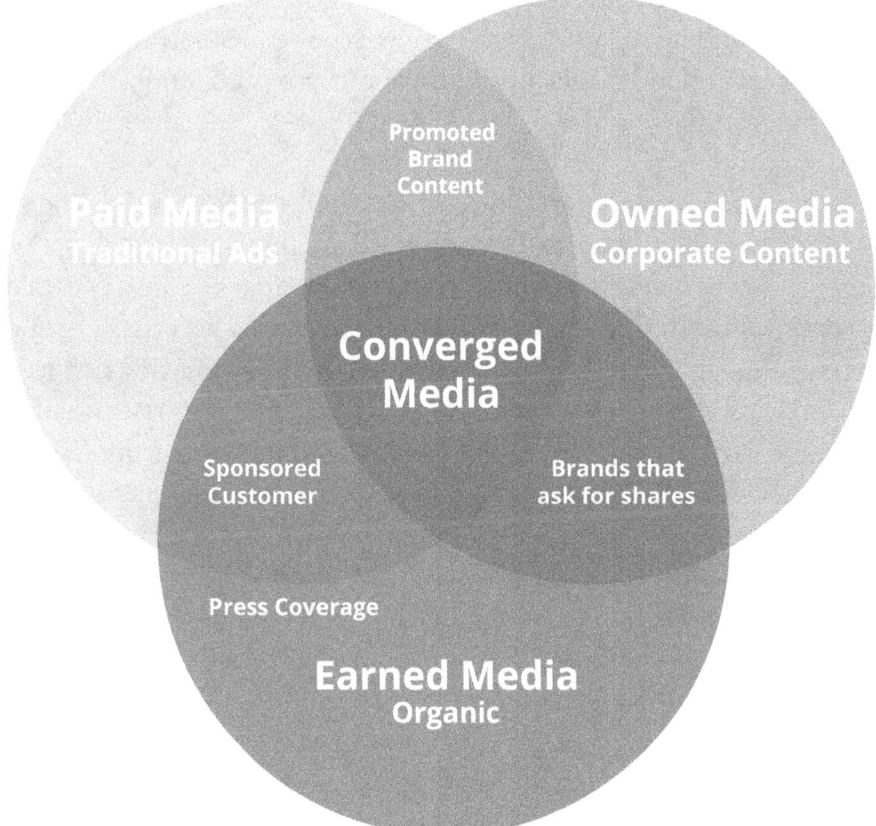

Figure 28. The Converged Media Imperative: How Brands Must Combine Paid, Owned & Earned Media, Source: Altimeter Group, 2012.

1. **Paid Media** – Advertising, such as magazine advertising, sponsored content, display ads, PPC ads, price comparators, and other types.
2. **Earned Media** – Looks like traditional public relations, resulting from public, media, blogging, and influencer methods of promotion.
3. **Owned Media** – Media that you own, ranging from blogs and your website to papers: The main focus of your content marketing efforts.
4. **Shared Media** – Shared content, referrals, community-driven content, reviews, and, where the first three overlap, promoted brand content, sponsored customers, and brands that ask for shares.
5. **Converged Media** – All of the above four categories combined and integrated create a new type of promotion. It is less about media, but more about cross channel integration.

No single type of medium can stand alone and be successful. Therefore, it is essential to converge all types of media.

If you want to acquire customers for your business of any type, take in to consideration that the customer journey is always cross channel and never linear. Therefore, the dynamic customer journey needs to be taken into consideration. In the center of the customer-centric view stands the fact that no medium or channel should be disconnected, which is different from a channel-by-channel view because our content, media, and channels merely serve as a way to accomplish business goals. The main factor driving all our efforts should be actual customer experience and every point of contact with our business, no matter of types of media and channels that create it.

Good marketing is always integrated marketing.

Organic content promotion increases the visibility of your content and the efficiency of your marketing campaigns without spending money on ads.

Just a few of the most effective organic content promotion methods are:

* Web pages, articles, and blogs entries
* Guest blogs
* Email marketing
* Webinars
* Influencers
* Videos
* How-to guides
* Case studies
* Infographics
* Customer reviews
* Streaming presentation
* User-generated content
* Interviews
* Customer support stories

The benefit of doing organic promotion is creating your brand authority on many potential platforms. Because you do not need a budget to do organic promotion, then you have no limitations to promoting more.

Increasing brand awareness is one of the crucial benefits of your organic promotion. Consistency plays a vital role in promoting your content, both for brand recognition and satisfying social media and search engine algorithms.

One of the main channels for paid promotions is search engine ads on search platforms and paid social media campaigns on social media.

Paid promotions are best to deliver highly targeted content to the public that will find your content useful. Paid promotions depend on budgets to achieve results. Testing is essential at first in paid promotions, in order not to waste your budget on poorly performing paid campaigns.

The best results will be achieved when you use paid promotion on your best performing organic content. So, bringing both types of promotions together will bring you the best results.

On search engine pages, such as Google, it is harder to choose which is good content to promote. Therefore, you need to check what performs well and then decide whether to promote it. Social media platforms will propose paid promotion on high performing organic content.

Promoting content should attract new users to your pages. If you are not getting new users to your pages, that is a reliable indicator that promotion is not performing well.

Customizing messages for each channel is essential, always test the performance of promoting content on a smaller budget, before you invest a more substantial sum.

THE HOOK MODEL: BUILDING A HABIT

Why does some social media content become viral? And why does some social media become addictive to users? We can dare to say that social media is designed in such a way to create a habit using the "Hook Model".

The definition of a habit is behavior that is done without too much thinking.

Social media has habit-forming potential, which is one of the aspects of their digital innovation, next to constant availability for communication.

THE HOOK MODEL

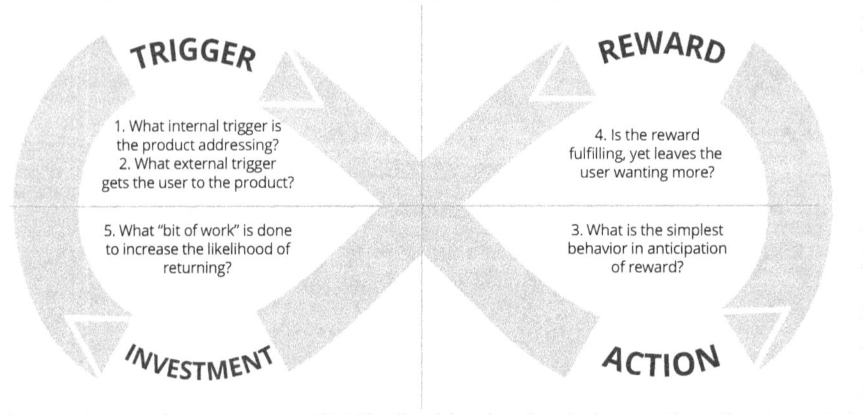

Figure 29. The Hook Model. Source: *Hooked*, **Nir Eyal**

Consumer psychologist Nir Eyal developed the "Hook Model" in his book *Hooked*. He created his four-step model by researching common traits between successful products, using insights from behavioral psychology and neuroscience, and combining it with his personal experience in the advertising industry.

The Hook is a process that companies use to "catch" consumers, so dealing with their business will become a habit for them. Such consumers will also become brand ambassadors that will bring new users by word-of-mouth at little or no cost at all.

The four stages of the Hook Model are: trigger, action, variable reward, investment.

There are external and internal triggers that cause people to carry out the desired action, and that action happens because people expect rewards.

External triggers are the ones where information about what to do next is within the trigger (emails, billboards, other).

Internal triggers are the ones where the information for what to do next is formed through an association in the user's memory (people, places, emotions, situations, routines).

People are more likely to develop such habits when they have to invest some time in going through the Hook process, because this forms the internal triggers and creates the impression that their work resulted in a reward. For many, and especially the younger generations, posting content on social media networks and receiving engagement from others is equal to real work in the real world.

Successful businesses and online communicators solve peoples' pain by formulating products and services as relief from pain points.

All companies can use the Hook Model to get consumers on board with their service and products. Once consumers are hooked, there is less need for marketing and advertising. Hooked consumers will advertise the business freely online by word-of-mouth.

The steps in the Hook Model, seen in the above diagram, are detailed below:

1. **Trigger: The Activator of Behavior**

Either external or internal, both are signs telling people what action they should take. When a person sees an external trigger, it will direct them to a particular action (for example, a login button on a web page is an online trigger).

External triggers can be one of four categories:

* **Earned** – Publicizing an event or creating a video with the hope of becoming viral.
* **Paid** – Buying advertising space to attract new users and convert them into loyal customers.
* **Relationship** – Such as word-of-mouth recommendations via social media, user forums, or other digital communication methods.
* **Owned** – After receiving users' permission, the company can push notifications to users. For example, to the smartphone of the user or their web-browser.

Internal triggers are subconscious associations between emotion and action or thought. For example, boredom will often drive you to check your email. People will often form habitual reactions to some experiences or pain points during their day. Businesses exploit users' pain points by offering comfort or solutions to their problems.

Businesses greatly benefit if they can understand which internal triggers cause people to use their products or services.

2. Action: Anticipation of a Reward

Action is what a trigger is trying to spark. When people act by habit, they act instinctively with almost no thought about it. In this case, action is how you behave because you expect a reward.

The actions that require little mental effort form habits. Social networks use a model where they identify human desires; usually the ones that exist for a long time, and then use steps of hooking to create a habit. Searching on Google doesn't take a lot of time or effort, so it becomes a habit for human beings to use it often.

3. Variable Reward: Creating Craving

The Hook Model builds desire by creating cravings. When people act, they experience the relief of solving their problem or satisfying their urge. Giving users variable instead of full rewards will create more needs.

Studies of reward mechanism behavior show that anticipation of a reward activates the brain's pleasure center. At the same time when people expect rewards, incentives start becoming less attractive. Introducing variable, unexpected, or intermittent rewards revives activity in the brain's pleasure center.

Variable rewards belong to one of the following types: the tribe, the hunt, and the self. Tribe rewards tap into the desire to connect socially and to feel included. Social media sites and computer games exploit this universal craving. People visit social media repeatedly to see if their friends "like" their posts. Games give users the chance to earn different types of badges in recognition of their achievements. Rewards of the hunt taps into search for material resources and information. Rewards of the self taps into search for intrinsic rewards of mastery, competence, and completion.

4. **Investment: The User Does Some Work**

When people invest more effort in their purchase of a product they desire, they become more committed, and even small investments of time or energy create bonds. For example, part of the appeal of IKEA is that you need to invest effort in assembling furniture, compared to when you purchase ready-made furniture. In most cases the effort is minimal, and the price reflects the fact that customers have to do some of the work themselves.

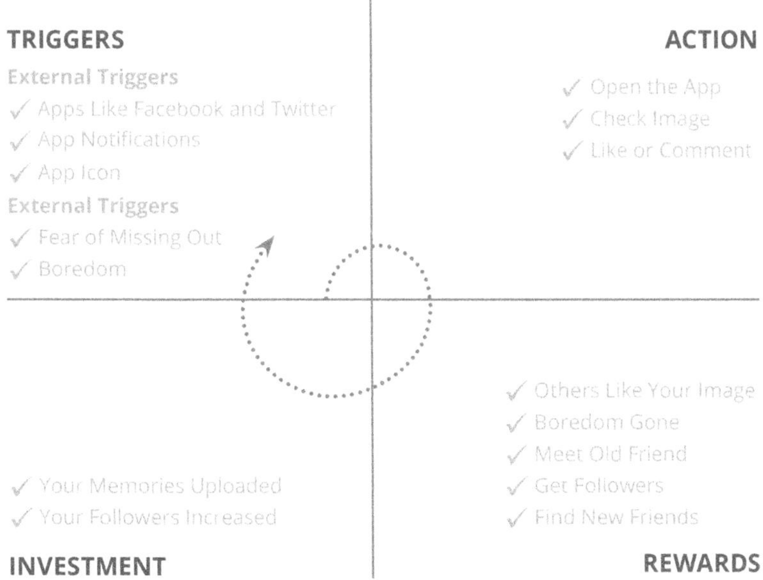

Figure 30. The Hook Model Canvas of social media networks

When people commit to behavior, it is highly likely they will repeat it in the future, if the reward is naturally positive.

For example, when users post their resumes on LinkedIn and use the time to add data to their profiles, it is unlikely they will switch to another similar site and repeat the sign-up process again.

The Hook Model is circular because external triggers encourage users to return, making their habits stronger each time.

Social media network sites are habits that most people use daily, precisely as their designers intended.

Creating a habit in your audience is equivalent to using paid promotions, and is often more efficient than any paid campaign. Digital personal brands with huge audiences function by creating habits through social media and their online presence. That is the secret of their appeal that makes audiences follow them and engage with any content they create.

AFTERWORD

By not stepping into your greatness, you are letting down everyone around you whom you can inspire, touch, or influence.

Amber Hurdle

YOU ALREADY HAVE A PERSONAL brand, and if you do not personally build and manage it, the people around you will do it for you. There is no bigger risk for your career and life than allowing other people to build your brand.

Personal branding is for the people that desire freedom from being overinfluenced by others.

Digital branding always stems out of authenticity and simple, effective communications. In the modern world personal branding brings influence.

When you understand digital personal branding, it becomes the most powerful tool in your career and life development.

Perception of your digital personal brand by your audience is your reality. What people perceive about you when you post and interact online becomes your reality. If people perceive you as good in your field of work, they will hire you more. By changing audience perception, you can create a new reality for yourself.

Personal branding is for everyone, not just famous, well-connected individuals. Personal branding is not complex, yet it requires effort.

Digital personal branding is not about pretending to be a perfect person; it is about being authentic in the world with all your flaws and strengths.

No one can tell your story better than you can; the best time to start telling your story is today.

Congratulations on completing the chapters of this book. You have moved forward, transforming your personal brand to be what it truly deserves.

You are now ready to start, manage, and grow your personal digital brand.

At *www.dariosipos.com/resources* you can find all the graphical guides mentioned in this book and additional resources.

The next steps are to continue building and implementing your plan, staying consistent. Regularly search for new ideas that could be valuable to your audience. Content will enable you to start a relationship with your audience, and assure them you are on their side as a guide to a better life.

Do you want to continue your personal branding journey? I would love to continue growing with you, so feel free to reach out to me on social networks, and be sure to check my website *www.dariosipos. com* for content that will help you in your growth.

Together we can transform your personal brand, so you are an influential presence and voice on the Internet, who people will trust and listen to above all others.

Sincerely,
Dario Sipos

GLOSSARY

Ad blocking	The blocking of web advertisements.
B2B	Businesses that sell products or provides services to other businesses.
B2C	Businesses that sell products or provides services to the end-user consumers.
Banner ad	A graphical web advertising unit.
Blog	A frequent, chronological publication of personal thoughts and web links.
Bounce rate	In web analytics, the percentage of visitors who leave after viewing a single page.
Call to action (CTA)	The part of a marketing message that attempts to persuade a person to perform a desired action.
Click-through-rate (CTR)	The average number of click-throughs per hundred ad impressions, expressed as a percentage.
Conversion rate	The percentage of visitors who take a desired action.
Cookie	Information stored on a user's computer by a website so preferences are remembered for future requests.
Cost per click (CPC)	The cost, or cost-equivalent, paid per click-through.
Customer acquisition cost	The cost associated with acquiring a new customer.
Description tag	A html tag used by web page authors to provide a description for search engine listings.

Domain name	The location of an entity on the Internet.
Forum	An online community where visitors may read and post topics of common interest.
Geo-targeting	A method of detecting a website visitor's location to serve location-based content or advertisements.
Inbound link	A link from a site outside of your site.
Inbound marketing	A marketing model whose sales performance relies on the initiative of its client base to find and purchase a product.
Keyword	A word used in performing a search.
Keyword research	The search for keywords related to your website, and the analysis of which ones yield the highest return on investment.
Link building	The process of increasing the number of inbound links to a website in a way that will increase search engine rankings.
Link popularity	A measure of the quantity and quality of sites that link to your site.
Marketing automation	The use of software to automate repetitive tasks related to marketing activities and connect different parts of the marketing funnel.
Marketing plan	The part of the business plan outlining the marketing strategy for a product or service.
Meta tags	Tags to describe various aspects about a web page.
Organic search	The unpaid entries in a search engine results page that were derived based on their contents' relevance to the keyword query.
Outbound link	A link to a site outside of your site.
Pop-up ad	An ad that displays in a new browser window.

Return on investment (ROI)	The ratio of profits (or losses) to the amount invested.
Search engine	A program that indexes documents, then attempts to match documents relevant to the users' search requests.
Search engine optimization (SEO)	The process of choosing targeted keyword phrases related to a site, and ensuring that the site places well when those keyword phrases are part of a web search.
Search retargeting	The use of a site visitor's search history as a basis for the ads that the visitor will see.
SERP	Shorthand for a page of search engine results, typically the first page of organic listings.
Social networking	The process of creating, building, and nurturing virtual communities and relationships between people online.
Spam	Inappropriate commercial message of extremely low value.
URL	The location of a resource on the Internet.
Vlog	A blog that publishes video content.
Website traffic	The number of visitors and visits a website receives.
Word-of-mouth marketing	A marketing method that relies on casual social interactions to promote a product.

TOOLS

Analytics
Alexa (*www.alexa.com*):
Internet analytics tool

Google Trends (*trends.google.com*):
Internet analytics tool

MOZ (*www.moz.com*):
Internet analytics tool

SEMRush (*www.semrush.com*):
Internet analytics tool

SimilarWeb (www.similarweb.com):
Internet analytics tool

Google's marketing services and external sources.

Asset Depositories
Promo (*www.promo.com*):
Largest depository of promotional videos

ThemeForest (*www.themeforest.net*):
Largest depository of WordPress Themes

Domain Research
KnowEm (*www.knowem.com*)

Namechk (*www.namechk.com*)

Graphics Editing Online Software
Canva (canva.com)

Pablo by Buffer (*pablo.buffer.com*)

Keyword Research

Google Ads (*ads.google.com*)

Google Trends (*trends.google.com*)

Keywordtool (*www.keywordtool.io*)

News and PR
PRUnderground (*www.prunderground.com*):
Affordable Online Press Release distribution service to Google News, social media, and 100+ news and TV websites

Right Relevance (rightrelevance.com):
Aggregator of news for use in content creation

Plagiarism Checker

Copyscape (*www.copyscape.com*)

Recognition
Awardshub (*www.awardshub.com*):
Find opportunity for rewards

Search
Pipl (*www.pipl.com*)

Social Searcher (*www.social-searcher.com*)

Social Media Calendar Software
Buffer (*www.buffer.com*)

Hootsuite (*www.hootsuite.com*)

Speaking Opportunities
Speakerhub (*www.speakerhub.com*)

Speakermatch (*www.speakermatch.com*)

Writing and Spelling
Grammarly (*www.grammarly.com*)

RESOURCES AND FURTHER READING

Nir Eyal with Ryan Hoover. *Hooked: How to Build Habit-Forming Products*. Portfolio Penguin, 2014.

Donald Miller. *Building a Story Brand: Clarify your message so customers will listen*. Harper Collins Leadership, 2017.

'The Converged Media Imperative: How Brands Must Combine Paid, Owned & Earned Media'. Altimeter Group, 2012.

HubSpot.com Inbound Marketing Resources

Brian Tracy. *Maximum Achievement: Strategies and Skills that Will Unlock Your Hidden Powers to Succeed*. Simon & Schuster, 2011.

Dan Ariely. *Predictably Irrational, Revised and Expanded Edition: The Hidden Forces That Shape Our Decisions*. Harper Perennial, 2010.

Dario Sipos website (*www.dariosipos.com*): Downloadable infographics and other useful marketing materials.